CW00566503

The
GREAT GATES
of
NORFOLK

WRITTEN AND ILLUSTRATED BY

Peter Kent

A *true* history of the gates of Norfolk, medieval and
modern, decorative and defensive, with sundry
associated tangential details

CUPOLA

The Great Gates of Norfolk
Published by Cupola Books
Text and illustrations: Peter Kent
Design: Johnson Design
Editor: Miles Mark

Printed in England by Page Bros, Norwich

ISBN 978-0-9933451-1-1

Cupola Books
27 Cambridge Street
Norwich
NR2 2BA
01603 614646
cupolabooks@icloud.com

A CIP catalogue record for this book is available
from the British Library.

This book is number ___619___
of a limited edition of 1000.
The first 50 are signed and have an
original drawing here.
Numbers 50 to 200 are signed only.

Back Cover: 44 Nunnery Gate, Thetford

✤ CONTENTS ✤

30 Town Gaol, King's Lynn

34 East Lodge, Hillingdon

55 The Water Gate, Norwich

37 Castle Acre Priory

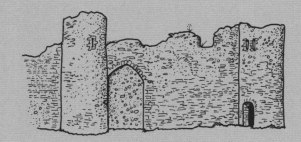

58 Claxton Castle, Claxton

41 Palmer's Lodge, Holkham

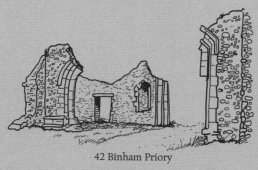

42 Binham Priory

29 Whitefriars Gate, King's Lynn

28 Austin Friars Gate, King's Lynn

✤ INTRODUCTION ✤

Gates are security made manifest. They are both utilitarian and symbolic as they form a barrier between the private and public world: between the domain of order within and the chaos outside, between the familiar and the unknown. At their humblest, the simple garden gate, they simply mark the passage from pavement to path and, with the click of their latches and the squeaking of their hinges, give advance warning of the postman, long expected guest or leaflet-bearing stranger. At their most forbidding, topped with razor wire and scanned by cameras, they deny entry to the unbidden and advertise that there is something of value on the other side that must be guarded and not unknowingly shared.

It is at the point of entry through the defences, a low privet hedge or great fortified wall, that the architectural vision is displayed. The gate is the expression of what lies within the wall; it is both advertisement and clue.

Norfolk has a great number of wonderful gates of all sorts; some, like that of Castle Acre, are simply functional; others, like the towering brick portal of Oxburgh Hall, combine defensive qualities with a bravura display of prestige and power; while many are almost purely decorative. Towns, castles, monasteries and stately homes, all had their gates, large numbers of which still survive, though many have been demolished as society has moved both physically and metaphorically towards a more open aspect. The gates of Norwich, Yarmouth and King's Lynn were not removed just because they restricted traffic; by the beginning of the 19th century their symbolic and military functions were as outworn and decayed as their fabric.

The gate, in its capacity as threshold, to a town or grand house was the place where the great and good arrived with pomp and ceremony, where the victorious entered in triumph and the defeated slunk away. Kings and queens, pilgrims and prisoners have all passed, and still pass, beneath the arches of Norfolk's gates. Religious pilgrims are much rarer now than in medieval times but are still to be seen in Walsingham plodding barefoot through the priory gate. Their modern, usually sensibly shod, counterpart is the tourist armed with camera and guidebook, who still visits and admires the surviving great gates as their builders intended.

This book contains some of the lesser known gates as well as others sadly demolished, along with their history and the tales of the exotic novelists, moped-riding clergymen, hunchbacked creators of priest's holes and fake Austrian archdukes associated with them. Read all about them here. Then follow in the footsteps of the great, the good, the mad and the bad to wonder at the great gates of Norfolk.

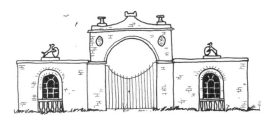

59 Chedgrave Lodge, Langley

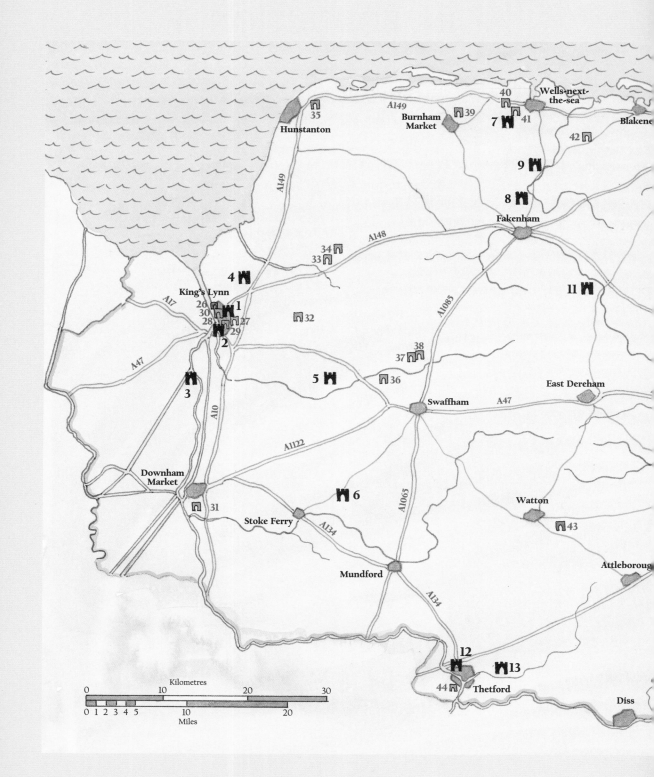

Kilometres

0   10   20   30

0 1 2 3 4 5   10   20

Miles

N

1 EAST GATE, KING'S LYNN

 KING'S LYNN'S MEDIEVAL FORTIFICATIONS consisted of a length of wall, an earth rampart with a palisade and a moat on three sides of the town with the river on the west. The East or St Catherine's was one of the town's five gates in the defences, standing on the bank of the Gaywood River where the road from Fakenham entered the town.[1] First built in the thirteenth century it was remodelled in the 1440s to make a very imposing structure with two corner turrets, a barbican and a drawbridge. As well as its defensive purpose this was also the point where tolls were collected on goods entering the town.

The gate played an important part in the siege of 1643; from it the garrison boldly sallied out to burn the almshouses at Gayton in case they provided cover to the besiegers. At the end of the siege, after terms of surrender were agreed, the Earl of Manchester feared the defenders might revoke their decision and drew up his army in the meadows outside the East Gate, announcing he would enter the town at once. The soldiers assumed 'a posture as might be most terrible to the enemy' by beating drums and blowing trumpets. An officer marched to the gate and demanded it be opened, but was told that was impossible and the army must enter one by one through the wicket. This was agreed but then a mob who wanted to fight on defied entry. There was a tense parley that lasted two hours, until a disgruntled defender on the wall by the gate called out, 'Give fire!' The credulous Parliamentary troops were mainly inexperienced novices and the dreaded words spread panic. The ranks broke and soldiers fled in all directions, falling off their horses or into ditches. Eventually order was restored, the mob dispersed and the victorious army marched in to take possession of the town.

During the eighteenth century the gate became dilapidated and the low arch was a serious hindrance to traffic; a wagon with a tall load of hay could not pass through. So in 1779 there was great embarrassment when a train of carts arrived carrying the picture collection from Houghton Hall on its way to the quay to be loaded on a ship bound for St Petersburg.[2] The huge canvases, including Rembrandts and Van Dyks, were in crates stacked vertically and most were too tall to pass beneath the arch. They had to be unloaded and carried through by hand. After that debacle the gate was doomed but another twenty-one years elapsed before it was finally demolished. Much of the stone was bought by the ffolkes family and taken to Hillingdon Hall to build the gateway which can still be seen from the A148. 🁢

---

1 The others were The South Gate, Douce Hill Gate and North and South Guanock Gates.
2 204 great canvases had been sold by the 3rd Earl of Orford for £40,550 to Catherine the Great of Russia.

Jonas Hanway, in 1769 the first man in England to carry an umbrella, was reviled and mocked; by 1800 the public had accepted its convenience and the umbrella passed without remark even in King's Lynn.

The front of the gate was faced with ashlar limestone; the inner side was built with cheaper local carrstone. The five loopholes on the first storey were designed for both longbows and crossbows. The three large cruciform loopholes make an impressive decorative feature as well as being functional. The small apertures on the second and third storeys were for small handguns. As well as the stout doors there was also a portcullis. Nothing of the gate remains but there is a short stretch of the town wall to the north and the old bridge still survives under the modern concrete one.

2 SOUTH GATE, KING'S LYNN

 THE SOUTH GATE OF KING'S LYNN is one of only two surviving town wall gates in Norfolk.[1] Despite its present squalid setting it is still an impressive entrance to the town. Dating from the thirteenth century it was rebuilt in its present form in 1437 and refaced in 1520.

It played its part in the siege of King's Lynn in 1643. This was the only major action of the Civil War in Norfolk, although it was a very unbloody affair compared to the battles and sieges in the rest of the country.[2] When war broke out in 1642 Norfolk was enthusiastic for Parliament but Lynn's support was lukewarm, and grew cooler as the war progressed. The Royalists in the town gained control and appointed Sir Hamon L'Estrange of Hunstanton Hall governor and commander of the town's forces. A Royalist army was in Lincolnshire but only after Parliament had paid for strengthening Lynn's fortifications did Sir Hamon declare for the King and close the gates on 28th August, 1643.

Sir Hamon hoped the Royalists would soon come to Lynn's relief but the town was quickly surrounded by the Earl of Manchester's army. Siege guns were brought to bombard the town. Mortar shells exploded, causing much terror but little damage, and an 18-pound cannonball crashed through the west window of St Margaret's church.[3]

After three weeks of bombardment and skirmishes, the Earl warned that Lynn would be stormed on 16th September and the garrison should send the women and children to safety. Faced with the prospect of an assault, fearing the resulting plunder and with no prospect of relief, the town council overruled Sir Hamon, who was still keen to fight, and asked for terms.

It was agreed that all arms and ammunition be surrendered, all prisoners freed and the Cavaliers from outside the town allowed to depart with their horses, swords and pistols. Ten shillings was to be paid to each Parliamentary soldier as compensation for being forbidden to plunder the town. Sir Hamon was held hostage until the terms were fulfilled but then allowed to return home where he remained unmolested for the rest of the war, still fulminating and plotting against Parliament.

Colonel Walton, Cromwell's brother in law, was made governor and the town was fortified with new earthworks in the modern bastioned style, to remain an impregnable Parliamentary fortress until the end of the war.

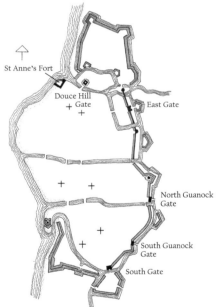

---

1 The other in Bailey Street, Castle Acre is a gate into the castle's outer bailey and not a true town gate.
2 Some accounts say 80 died but this is surely an exaggeration not supported by parish burial records. The true death toll was probably less than a dozen, possibly only three or four.
3 A cannonball, fired during the siege, hangs in the entrance archway of Hampton Court, Nelson Street.

The young George Vancouver (1757–1798), who found fame as an explorer of the north-west coast of America and after whom the Canadian city is named, gazes on the ooze and dreams of wide billowing oceans.

The South Gate was substantially rebuilt in 1520 when it was faced with ashlar masonry and the two large windows were inserted. The circular gunports date from the fifteenth century, though the handguns for which they were designed were obsolete by the sixteenth. There was a substantial stone bridge over the moat and a barbican. These were removed in the nineteenth century when two pedestrian passages were inserted at the base of the turrets and the bridge widened. The moat has now been filled in and the gate stands stripped of its defensive context, with one stream of traffic roaring through the arch and another beside it. The present setting is an ignoble and disgraceful way to display the finest town gate in the east of England.

3 ST MARY'S HALL, WIGGENHALL

 THERE ARE VERY FEW GREAT HOUSES in the Fens; the establishment of estates on reclaimed land took a different form to estates in the rest of the county. One is St Mary's Hall in Wiggenhall St Mary the Virgin, built in the mid sixteenth century for the Kervilles, who had held the manor on the banks of the Ouse since Norman times. Originally it was a brick mansion, rather like East Barsham, with an enclosed courtyard and an embattled and turreted gatehouse.

The hall did not last much longer than a single lifetime and was ruined by the mid-seventeenth century. The last of the Kervilles, Sir Henry was noted as a 'bigoted papist' and imprisoned in 1620 for hosting a meeting of fellow Catholics to discuss ways of helping the Holy Roman Emperor in his war against the King of Bohemia.[1] He died childless soon afterwards and the estate passed out of the family.[2] The house was allowed to decay; by the time Blomefield recorded it in the 1760s it was all demolished, apart from the gatehouse and stable block.

In 1864 the then Lord of the Manor, Gustavus Helsham, rebuilt the hall in a faithful imitation of the gatehouse's style with crenellations and corkscrew chimneys. He restored the gatehouse and converted the upper floor of the stable block into a ballroom with a glittering chandelier that descended from a recess in the roof.

This magnificence had somewhat decayed by 1983 when the hall was bought by the poet George MacBeth and his wife, the exotic and glamorous novelist, Lisa St Aubin de Terán. They moved to Wiggenhall from the equally flat marshlands of Oby where they had renovated the old rectory. Arriving in the Fens with a new baby and faced with another interminable restoration project it was hardly surprising that their marriage began to collapse along with the ceilings. St Aubin found the view from the mullioned windows particularly depressing.  *'For almost two years I had looked out across the bleak flatlands of the Fens, watching the bare treeless expanses of clay mud peppered only by scattered bungalows and the distant glint of the sugar factory chimney. It seemed ironic that I, who had once been the Queen of the Andes, with my endless miles of sugar cane and the tallest chimney in the state, should have come to fester in the long shadow of a steel sugar beet plant.'*[3]

She did not fester for long and soon moved to the more congenial climate and scenery of Umbria where, addicted to ruins, she began to renovate an old palazzo.

The hall remains in private hands; its drive barred by an elegant white wrought iron park gate. Gatehouse and hall lie hidden in trees. 🏰

---

1 James I's daughter, Elizabeth, had married Frederick V of the Palatine who became King of Bohemia in 1619 but was deposed by the Holy Roman Emperor in 1620. This was the start of the Thirty Years War between the Catholic Habsburgs and the Protestant states of Germany. James asked for a loan from the English nobility to support his son-in-law's cause. It is not surprising that Catholics should have objected.
2 He has a fine tomb in St Mary's church, surmounted by the hare that heads this page.
3 The sugar beet factory was about two miles to the north-east at Saddlebow in King's Lynn. It opened in 1927 and closed in 1997.

Miss Helsham sketches the ruined and romantic gate before it is restored and improved by her father.

The gatehouse has two octagonal three-storey towers flanking the entrance. There are no loopholes and the crenellations and general martial air is only for display. It could not have resisted serious attack. The large windows and generous provision of fireplaces indicate that the accommodation was comfortable, probably for a porter. There is a large public room over the gate where rents were collected and a manorial court held. This view is taken from Cotman's etching of 1818 when it was a romantic ruin. A single-storey porch was unfortunately added in the 1860s between the towers before the main gate.

4 CASTLE RISING

CASTLE RISING IS ONE OF THE FINEST Norman keeps in England, surrounded by substantial earthworks, but its history is distinguished only by its most infamous resident, Isabella, the She-Wolf of France and widow of the ill-fated Edward II. The castle was built around 1138 by William d'Aubigny, Earl of Arundel, who had extensive estates in Norfolk. The castle and its surrounding landscape were carefully planned, with a deer park, rabbit warren and model village, anticipating the works of Repton and Capability Brown by centuries.

There were three baileys, covering twelve acres, all surrounded by high earth banks and deep ditches. The great keep stands in the inner bailey, whose entrance is formed by the gatehouse and stone bridge. In the fourteenth century a wall was built along the top of the rampart, replacing a wooden stockade, and the gatehouse was rebuilt and enlarged.

Two uneventful centuries later, the castle was sold to Queen Isabella, who after the murder of her husband ruled England with her lover Roger Mortimer as regent for her young son Edward III. Edward seized power in 1330, executed Mortimer and imprisoned his mother in her own castle.

It was a very comfortable confinement. She had a generous income and maintained a regal state, with many servants, including minstrels and huntsmen. She lived in a range of now demolished buildings and kept the keep as a guest suite for important visitors, who included her son, the King of France and her daughter Joan, the Queen of Scots. The tale that she went mad and paced the great hall with frantic steps is the invention of chroniclers desperate for anecdote.

When Isabella died in 1358 the castle passed to the Black Prince. In the 1370s it was made ready to resist a threatened French invasion and equipped with two small cannon but that was the last time it played a military role. In the fifteenth century it was used only as a hunting lodge and the buildings fell into disrepair. By the mid-sixteenth century it was derelict, when Henry VIII sold the property to Thomas Howard, the Duke of Norfolk, and most of the buildings were demolished. It was not until the nineteenth century, when Mary and Fulke Greville Howard inherited the property, that the castle was renovated, restored and opened to the public. 🏰

The gatehouse in *c.*1200

The gatehouse in *c.*1400

Queen Isabella returns to the castle after a stroll in the outer bailey.

The gate to the inner bailey was built at the same time as the keep, with a stone bridge across the dry ditch. It was originally a simple structure without any flanking towers. It may have had a drawbridge as well as a portcullis and strong doors. When the wall along the top of the earth rampart was built in the fourteenth century, the gate tower was raised in height and two walls built out to form a barbican. It is very ruined now and its original form is not obvious.

5 PENTNEY PRIORY GATE

 PENTNEY PRIORY WAS A SMALL MONASTERY of Augustinian canons on the bank of the river Nar, a mile west of the village. It was founded by Robert De Vaux in about 1130 and quietly went about its good works of prayer, charity and education until the sixteenth century.

It was regularly visited by representatives of the bishop to check that all was well and, apart from the odd minor complaint, was always judged satisfactory. Then in 1535 the process to suppress the monasteries began. Although the public policy was to only reform religious houses, the hidden aim was to close them and confiscate their wealth. Thomas Cromwell sent out commissioners to examine every religious community and report on their conduct. Not surprisingly the reports were usually damning.

Two commissioners, Thomas Legh and John ap Rice came to Pentney in 1534 and at first found little fault in the prior, Robert Codde, and his twelve canons. There was one complaint about the state of repairs and the competence of the schoolmaster but that was all. Once they had left, Legh and ap Rice wrote a secret and unlikely report in which they accused Prior Codde of having an affair with the abbess of Marham and five canons of regularly breaking their vow of chastity.

A few months later the local county commissioners visited Pentney to assess its wealth. As they were local gentry and not direct employees of Cromwell, they reported that the canons were 'alle Prystes of very honest name and goode religious persones who doue desyre the kynges highness to contynue and remayne in religione'. They wrote again to Cromwell, 'The prior relieved those quarters wondrously where he dwells, and it would be a pity not to spare a house that feeds so many indigent poor, which is in a good state, maintains good service, and does so many charitable deeds.'

This was not enough and the priory was closed in 1537. The canons and their eighty-three servants were sent out into the world and an uncertain future.[1] The buildings and contents were sold to the Earl of Rutland and all but the gatehouse eventually demolished. By the end of the nineteenth century it was a roofless ruin but in 2011 was beautifully restored and now functions as a wedding venue, a little ironic given its monastic origins.

---

1 But not Robert Codde. He was awarded an annual pension of £24 and made the warden of St Giles Hospital in Norwich.

The bridesmaids arrive too late for the wedding, their driver having neglected to recharge his sat-nav device, not because of a shortage of lamp oil. (Matthew 25: 1–13)

The imposing gatehouse was built between 1380 and 1425 and is a smaller version of the gate of Thornbury Abbey in Lincolnshire. The materials are flint, carrstone, brick and some ashlar. The gate passage was originally vaulted. The brick chimney flues were added in the fifteenth century. It was never a serious fortification although there is a loophole in the ground floor of each of the turrets.

6 OXBURGH HALL

EDMUND BEDINGFIELD GAINED A LICENCE to fortify his house in 1482 from King Edward IV and the result was the stupendous brick gatehouse, probably the best example of its kind. It was one of the first great houses in England to be built in brick, then a novel and expensive material. In a county that was strongly Protestant and pro-Parliament Oxburgh was an island of contrariness. The Bedingfields were both staunch Catholics and loyal Royalists. They stood against the Reformation and during all the dangerous years of the 1580s and 90s when Catholics were persecuted and priests hunted, Oxburgh was a safe haven. The Bedingfields maintained a chaplain and, although denounced for harbouring papists and fined, nothing worse happened.

During the Civil War Sir Henry Bedingfield and his sons fought for the King and suffered great financial loss and imprisonment for their allegiance. The house was badly damaged by Parliamentary troops and the estate ravaged but, unlike many Royalists, the fortunes of the family eventually recovered.

There must have been visiting priests in the dangerous years because, should they have needed to hide, two priest's holes were installed. One of these survives in the staircase of the gatehouse. It is a small chamber, entered from the stair by a pivoting trap door, and very cramped, with nothing more than a bench and a small hole through which the hidden priest could be fed. This was a necessary precaution as searches could last for days or even weeks and some priests died of starvation or suffocation.

The Oxburgh priest's hole was almost the certainly the work of Nicholas Owen[1], a joiner by trade and Jesuit by vocation, who made many secret places in Catholic houses. He was the acknowledged master of this clandestine craft and his work saved many lives, although there is no evidence that his hiding place at Oxburgh was ever put to the test. The second priest's hole in the Great Hall was destroyed along with the hall itself. Blomefield enthused that it was 'justly accounted one of the best old Gothick halls in England' but this did not save it from the modernising urge of Sir Richard Bedingfield, who pulled it down in 1775. The Victorian Bedingfields atoned by thoroughly gothicising what remained and making Oxburgh the picturesque house we see today. Apparently a very young Pugin was appointed to restore the house but he does not seem to have done much.

The final blow to the Bedingfields was the high taxation of the late 1940s and they made Oxburgh over to the National Trust in 1952 although they still manage to live in part of it.

---

1 Owen was born in Oxford and became the servant of the Jesuit Fr. John Gerard. Owen was captured and died on the rack in the Tower of London in 1606. He was made a saint in 1970.

A Cavalier, Roundhead and uncommitted wench take a photograph of themselves after a Civil War re-enactment in the grounds of the hall.

The polygonal towers rise to a height of 85 feet. Decorated brick friezes divide the towers into seven tiers but inside there are only three storeys. The parapet between the two towers rests on machicolations through which stones, boiling water or quicklime could be dropped on attackers battering at the gate. That Edmund Bedingfield was rich enough to possess guns is evidenced by the rather unusual lower gunports flanking the gate. These consist of a cross-slit running down to a stirrup-shaped aperture, a type common in Germany; perhaps their presence here is due to Oxburgh's proximity to King's Lynn, with its Hanseatic connections.

7 THE TRIUMPHAL ARCH, HOLKHAM

THE TRIUMPHAL ARCH AT HOLKHAM HALL commemorated no great victory but it did overlook the first mock battle and review of the Volunteers in Norfolk. The Volunteer movement began after the invasion scare of 1859 when, to increase the army without expense, the Government authorised the formation of corps of riflemen. There was great enthusiasm. Thousands flocked to enrol and Tennyson wrote an encouraging poem.[1]

In Norfolk the Norwich Rifle Corps was the first to be formed, with units in the county quickly following. One of the attractions of the Volunteers was that they could choose their own uniforms; the Norfolk units adopted a grey coat and trousers with black braiding and belt. Men had to pay for their uniforms; rifles were provided by the Government. There was an annual subscription of a guinea (£1.05) and six hours drill a week.

The first public parade was in October 1859 but it was not until September 1861 that a grand review at Holkham Hall was organised. 1,700 enthusiastic amateur soldiers arrived by train from Norwich, Yarmouth, Brandon and King's Lynn. However, moving such large numbers proved beyond the capacity and competence of the Eastern Counties Railway and most were too late for the military programme to begin on time. The display was scheduled for 11am but did not start until 2.15pm. The programme had to be curtailed. Before a crowd of 20,000 spectators and to the music of three bands, the Volunteers marched in column, wheeled and countermarched before deploying in line to make a mock attack on the woods in the park. The spectators were delighted by the crackle of musketry and the dense clouds of smoke.

The troops were reviewed by Major-General Sir Archdale Wilson, a Norfolk man and hero of the Indian Mutiny, who congratulated them before dismissing them to a generous lunch provided by the Earl of Leicester. Two tons of beef and mutton, 600 bottles of wine and ample supplies of bread and beer were consumed before the Volunteers gave three cheers for the Earl and marched through the staterooms of Holkham Hall before setting out for the railway station at Wells.

The Eastern Counties Railway proved even worse at removing the crowds than in bringing them. There were not enough carriages. The telegraph broke down, so trains queued for hours on the single line. A tired and frustrated mob milled about the station at Wells, storming each train as it arrived. The Yarmouth artillery contingent 'behaved disgracefully in a most unsoldierly manner', firing their rifles inside the carriages, swearing abominably and drinking copiously. Many of the Norwich corps did not reach the city until six in the morning of the following day. It would have been, as an enraged correspondent to the *Norwich Mercury* pointed out, quicker to march.

---

1 'Form, Form, Riflemen Form! Ready, be ready to meet the storm! Riflemen, Riflemen, Riflemen form!'

Captain Crimpleton of the King's Lynn Volunteers begins to lose hope that the rest of his company will arrive in time to take their part in the battle.

The Triumphal Arch was designed by William Kent in 1739 and completed in 1752 by Matthew Brettingham who omitted Kent's pyramid-like obelisks over the side arches, probably on grounds of cost. It is built of yellow gault brick with unusual whole-flint rustication that gives a massive appearance without the expense of stone. The arch was meant as a striking landmark, to impress visitors as they approached the Hall along the artfully designed southern avenue. Until the coming of the railway to Wells this was the principal route for visitors from London. There are two more gates into the park: the imposing Tudor North Gate leading into the village and the Palladian Palmer's Lodge on Golden Gates Drive.

8 EAST BARSHAM MANOR

EAST BARSHAM MANOR, all mellow old bricks, mullioned windows, corkscrew chimneys and pepper pot finials, is every calendar publisher's idea of a Tudor house. One of the best sixteenth-century prodigy houses standing, it ought to be better known, and would be, if owned by the National Trust and within easy reach of London. Although irresistible and delightful, it is not altogether authentic. The great gate and chimneys were repaired but the west end – on the other side from the gatehouse – was rebuilt completely, with only the original facade and chimneys kept. The work was conscientious and only the most expert eye can detect the new from the original.

East Barsham, or Wolterton, Manor was built for Sir Henry Fermor in about 1520–30.[1] He had no great estates but a lucrative position at court; the house was to display his wealth and status. It has often been stated that Henry VIII stayed at East Barsham while on a pilgrimage to Walsingham but, much as we might like to imagine this, chronology points out its impossibility.[2]

For such an extraordinary house East Barsham has very little history. The Fermors lived uneventfully there and passed it on through marriage to the Calthorpes, who passed it to the L'Estranges, who in their turn passed it to the Astleys. None seemed to cherish it very much and by the eighteenth century, when its style was thoroughly out of fashion, most of it was ruined and the remainder used as a farmhouse. It still had admirers though, drawn to its romantic desolation. Humprey Repton, the landscape designer and architect, visited in 1808 and wrote, 'During a late tour of Norfolk I saw the remains of an old manor house which I believe in richness of moulded brickwork exceeds anything of the kind in England.' The antiquarian Walter Rye in the 1870s also wondered why it was still an unloved ruin. By then Tudorbethan was very much in fashion but there were quite enough fine houses around and the county gentry were feeling the pinch of the agricultural depression.

It was not until after the first world war that it changed hands yet again. Restoration began in 1919 for a Mr Coleman but was finished by the exotically styled Count Francis Jeremie Habsburg-Lothringen, who claimed to be the grandson of an Austrian archduke.[3] The mysterious count lived in the house for only three years, amusing himself by playing darts with the locals and roaring round the lanes in a sports car. He disappeared abruptly in 1938 after being declared bankrupt and then jumping bail before his trial for defrauding Fortnum and Mason.

---

1   There is no documentary evidence for its building although Blomefield, on a visit in the 1740s, found the date 1538 inscribed on a beam.
2   Henry made his only pilgrimage to Walsingham in January 1511 to give thanks to Our Lady of Walsingham for the birth of his first son – who died several weeks later.
3   The count was unknown to the *Almanach de Gotha*. He was really a Lincolnshire farmer called Jeremy Willoughby.

The counterfeit count takes a last fond look at his mansion before fleeing his creditors.

The gatehouse of Castle Rising was built for defence; the gatehouse of Oxburgh Hall for defence and display; the elaborate gatehouse of East Barsham for display only. It pretends to be martial. The two polygonal buttresses pose as flanking towers and the decoration below the battlements suggests machicolation. The archway is of moulded brick, as are the very prominent royal arms. Count Habsburg-Lothringen added the lions on the gateposts. They bear the cross of Lorraine or, in German, Lothringen.

9 WALSINGHAM PRIORY GATE

 A CITY TODAY NEEDS AN 'ICONIC' MUSEUM to put it on the tourist map; in the Middle Ages shrines drew the crowds and Walsingham was England's premier shrine, so popular it was said the Milky Way guided the pilgrims there.

It all began in 1061 when Lady Richeldis had a vision of the Virgin Mary, who asked her to recreate the house where the Annunciation took place. Richeldis built a small wooden hut in which she placed a statue of Mary and pilgrims came – at first in dozens, later in thousands. The Holy House was enclosed in a vast church, the statue was encrusted with jewels and gold and the adjoining priory of Augustinian canons grew rich on the pilgrims' gifts.

In 1538 Henry VIII cast his covetous eyes on Walsingham, despite having been a pilgrim. The priory was closed, pillaged and demolished. The venerated statue was burnt in London and only the east end of the church and the gate survived. Walsingham was then forgotten until 1896 when a Roman Catholic convert bought and restored the Slipper Chapel[1] at Houghton St Giles in an attempt to revive the shrine. Several small pilgrim bands came before the Catholic authorities lost interest.[2]

Then, in 1922, the Anglican vicar of Walsingham, the dizzily High Church Revd Hope Paten, set up a statue of Our Lady of Walsingham in the parish church and large numbers of Anglo-Catholic pilgrims came to venerate it. By the end of the decade there were so many that Hope Paten built the small, vaguely Italianate Shrine Church[3] outside the priory wall. In 1931 the statue was solemnly translated from the parish to the Shrine Church and even more pilgrims came. Alarmed by this, the Roman Catholics revived their shrine at Houghton St Giles. In 1934 the Slipper Chapel was made the National Shrine of Our Lady and, until relations between the two churches improved, Walsingham was beset by rival bands of pilgrims.

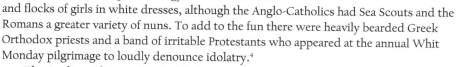

To an outsider it was difficult to tell the two Catholic species apart. Both deployed forests of banners, squads of surpliced clergy, columns of nuns and flocks of girls in white dresses, although the Anglo-Catholics had Sea Scouts and the Romans a greater variety of nuns. To add to the fun there were heavily bearded Greek Orthodox priests and a band of irritable Protestants who appeared at the annual Whit Monday pilgrimage to loudly denounce idolatry.[4]

The Anglican Shrine Church, filled with candles and lace-draped statues, was more 'Catholic' than the Roman Catholics' Slipper Chapel which was self-consciously medieval in style. All these differences have now largely disappeared and, although the Anglo-Catholic faction in the Church of England is now a guttering candle, Walsingham seems to thrive.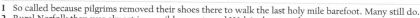

---

1 So called because pilgrims removed their shoes there to walk the last holy mile barefoot. Many still do.
2 Rural Norfolk then was almost impossibly remote and Walsingham's only communication was by infrequent trains on a small branch line. Most Roman Catholics then lived in the North-West, the Midlands and London and would have found it very difficult to get there. It was the development of motor coaches and better roads that made mass pilgrimage to Walsingham possible.
3 Designed by Milner & Craze, it was sited on what Hope Paten wrongly claimed was the site of the Holy House. When the foundations were dug an old well was discovered which was immediately incorporated into the church as a holy well. There is also a slim campanile, a reminder of Hope Paten's many holidays in Italy.
4 These are members of the Protestant Truth Society founded in 1889 by John Kensit and sometimes known as the Kensitites. Their mission is to prevent the spread of Catholic practices in the Church of England. They used to prosecute clergymen for using Catholic rituals and smash up churches with too many statues and candles but now content themselves with shouting at pilgrims.

Holy gridlock at the priory gate as three pilgrim bands uncharitably contest the right of way. Can you tell the Anglo from the Roman Catholics?

The gatehouse of the priory in the High Street was built in the mid-fifteenth century of flint dressed with stone. It has lost its crenellated parapet, the statuary on the facade and the vaulting in the passage; however, it is still a magnificent structure. Modern pilgrims still pass through on special occasions, treading in the (bare) footsteps of medieval kings and peasants, although the original Holy House is no more than a grass bump in the lawn. The original door was set across the middle of the passage between the two arches. Unlike many such gates there was never a special pedestrian entrance.

10 BACONSTHORPE CASTLE

 BACONSTHORPE CASTLE IS A TYPICAL EXAMPLE of a manor built in the troubled times of the mid-fifteenth century when the best way to secure your property was to fortify it. The castle was completed in about 1486 but in ruins two hundred years later. Its rise and fall mirrors the fortunes of the Heydon family who began their rise to political and social prominence during the Wars of the Roses. John Heydon was a skilled and ruthless lawyer who conveniently forgot to obtain a royal licence to crenellate an existing small manor house which he transformed into a fortress of some strength.

The castle was square, with tall flint walls flanked by five small turrets on the west side, and a larger tower at the north-east corner, and surrounded by a wide water-filled moat. Inside was a large hall and a range of domestic buildings. The main strength of the castle was in the gatehouse which was intended as a defensible keep if the walls were breached. The Heydons were rich enough to not only furnish their private quarters with feather beds and curtains but to have an armoury that included small guns for which special loopholes were installed. In 1560 the outer courtyard and its gatehouse was built but this was mainly for display and added little to the strength of the defences.

During the Armada scare of 1588 Sir William Heydon was the commander of the local troops and Baconsthorpe was the headquarters of the forces mustered to guard the vulnerable beaches at Weybourne, where extensive fortifications were planned, though probably not built.[1] That was the last time the castle had any military function. For the next fifty years Baconsthorpe was the centre of a large and prosperous sheep farm and the great hall was converted into a factory for spinning and weaving. One Christmas thirty shepherds were entertained to dinner, suggesting a combined flock of more than 20,000 sheep.

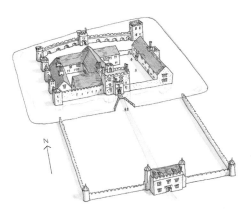

Alterations to the house were carried out in the early seventeenth century by Sir Christopher Heydon (1593–1623), but by this time the fortunes of the family were in decline. They were bad managers and heavily in debt. In the mid-seventeenth century most of the buildings on the moated site were demolished and the gatehouse and outer walls dismantled. Much of the stone was sold and carted away for use on the nearby Felbrigg estate.

The outer gatehouse was then known as Baconsthorpe Hall and in 1673 the last of the Heydons left and it passed to the egregiously named Zurishaddai Long.[2] It was occupied as an increasingly dilapidated farmhouse until 1920, when one of the pepper pot turrets collapsed and it was abandoned.

---

1 Baconsthorpe is shown on the map of the proposed fortifications drawn by Captain Edmund Yorke in May, 1588.
2 It means 'The Almighty is my rock and strength.' The name seems to have been more popular in Norfolk than in the Bible, where it occurs only once. In 1820 Baconsthorpe was owned by another Zurishaddai with the odd surname of Girdlestone. Zurishaddai Girdlestone! Sounds like a character from *Cold Comfort Farm*.

Had the Spanish landed it is unlikely that Baconsthorpe and its scratch garrison of parish militia could have resisted them for long.

The gatehouse was one of the first parts of the castle to be built of knapped flint and galetting (flint chips embedded in mortar) with stone quoins at the corners. The gate passages and adjoining chambers for porter and steward had elaborate stone vaulted roofs. There were three storeys with a two-storied porch. There was no portcullis and it is unlikely there was a drawbridge. It was comfortably equipped with fireplaces and privies. The large windows did not make it very defensible but these may be replacements. There are five unusual double loopholes in the adjoining wall.

11 STABLE COURT GATE, SENNOWE PARK

THERE ARE NOT MANY EDWARDIAN COUNTRY HOUSES in Norfolk. In the early twentieth century there were enough mansions for the established gentry and Norfolk was too far from London and the great northern cities to see new money found a country seat. Of Norfolk's Edwardian houses by far the grandest is Sennowe Park near Guist.[1]

It was built for Thomas Albert Cook, the grandson of the founder of the famous travel firm, who sold his share to his hardworking brothers, appropriately named Frank and Ernest, to live the life of a sporting country gentleman. Bert, as he was known, enthusiastically devoted his time to carriage driving – the most expensive and exclusive of equestrian sports – hunting, shooting, sailing and socialising.[2]

In 1904 Bert acquired Sennowe Hall, a small Georgian house in a lovely setting in the Wensum valley five miles east of Fakenham. He commissioned Norfolk's most distinguished architect, George Skipper,[3] then at the height of his powers, to remodel the existing house and went on a world tour – presumably organised by his brothers – while the builders were in.

When he returned the original house had been absorbed into a great mansion in Skipper's most exuberant baroque style. The cost of the house and remodelled grounds, which featured terraced Italianate gardens, pavilions, elaborate gate lodges, a grand drive with a wide, balustraded three-arch bridge across a dry valley and a romantic boathouse on an artificial lake, was prodigious – £76,000. The interior was lavish with ornate plasterwork, Corinthian columns and a barrel-vaulted library. (It is unlikely that Bert did much reading. He seems to have been an enthusiastic *bon viveur* with a lifestyle at odds with his family's temperance traditions.)[4] Instead of a ballroom there was a huge cast iron conservatory with a fountain and marble floor.

Skipper could not resist the indulgence of an enormous tower for the water supply. Built in the style of an Italian campanile, it housed a belfry, which chimed the quarter hours night and day. For a brief period, until complaints extinguished it, a powerful searchlight was mounted in the loggia at the top. Its beams lit up the lake for nocturnal duck shoots.

The house had a glittering period of only seven years. Bert died in 1914 and the straitened circumstances of post-war England meant it was no longer possible to run a house needing a staff of fifty. It is still lived in by the family and hosts film shoots, weddings and grand weekends. In the summer the park sometimes throbs to music or the roar of classic cars. In the hunting season the North Norfolk Harriers and the West Norfolk Foxhounds meet there in a convivial style of which Bert would surely approve.

1 Virtually all the big Edwardian houses in Norfolk are in North Norfolk near the coast e.g. Happisburgh, Overstrand, Kelling Hall and Voewood at Holt.
2 Once Bert drove a carriage and five horses in London's Hyde Park. When told it was illegal to drive a coach with a team of more than four horses he returned the next day with a coach, four horses and a mule. His yacht still survives and sails on the Broads today.
3 George John Skipper (1856–1948) designed the Royal Arcade and Norwich Union building in Norwich as well as several hotels in Cromer and the yacht club at Lowestoft.
4 The founder Thomas Cook's first excursion was conveying a temperance society from Leicester to Loughborough in 1841.

Bert Cooke practises with his carriage whip while the horses are readied in the stables behind.

The baroque gate to the Stable Court is a masterly display of exuberant architectural swagger. It is worthy of a Vauban fortress or Vanbrugh palace, making use of every baroque decorative device: unfluted Doric columns, cartouches, emphatic keystones, virile rustication, swags and palm leaves. The gate is the lavish expression of the affection that Bert had for his beloved coach-horses (whose names all began with S) and his dogs: two are carved in relief above the keystones of the side arches, while two more sit on guard on top of the inner columns. Behind the arch is a large coach house for carriages and extensive, beautifully tiled stables. There is a dovecote in the attic pediment as well as the obligatory stable clock housed in the copper-clad cupola.

12 THETFORD PRIORY GATE

THETFORD PRIORY WAS A MAJOR HOUSE of Cluniac monks, a very strict and austere branch of the Benedictine order, noted for the elaborate ceremonial of their services. They came to Thetford in 1104 when Roger Bigod, Earl of Suffolk, given two options to fulfil a vow, of either building a monastery or making an uncomfortable and dangerous pilgrimage to the Holy Land, not unsurprisingly chose the first. The people of Thetford who had just lost their cathedral when the bishopric was moved to Norwich were glad to help and the new priory was quickly established with twelve monks from Lewes.

The first prior Stephen was noted for his sanctity, but another prior of that name two hundred years later was notorious for his evil ways. He turned the priory into a house of debauchery, carousing night and day with his brothers Bernard, a knight, and Guiscard, whom the chronicler, Matthew Paris bafflingly described as 'a freakish clerk whose womb was become like a bottle'.[1] The bad prior Stephen received his just deserts in 1248 when he was stabbed to death by one of the monks who resented being posted back to the mother house at Cluny.

Luckily a vision and subsequent miracle restored the priory's reputation and finances. A local cobbler had a vision of the Virgin Mary who, as customary, asked for a chapel in her honour. The monks obliged with a wooden chapel but the Virgin returned to the cobbler to demand that it be built in stone. Rather than go to too much trouble the monks erected a shrine in an existing Lady Chapel. They installed a statue that had been in store and while cleaning it found a silver plate in the virgin's head. When this was removed the statue was found to be stuffed with relics.[2] Overnight the delighted monks had acquired a major relic collection which would prove a magnet for pious pilgrims.

The faithful flocked to the new shrine and miracles inevitably followed. The bedridden walked, the lame skipped, the blind saw and two children were raised from the dead. Such was the wealth generated by the shrine that the monks could afford a brand new Lady Chapel and to extend their choir by forty feet.

In 1536 the priory was visited by the commissioners Thomas Legh and Richard Leyton. There were seventeen monks but disappointingly very little evil – just one theft and unspecified 'uncleanness'– was uncovered. The priory was ordered to be suppressed but it had a powerful defender in its patron the Duke of Norfolk, many of whose family were buried there. He asked the King that the priory be converted into a parish church with a college of secular canons drawn from the existing monks. Henry agreed but soon changed his mind and insisted on the absolute dissolution of the priory which was sold to the Duke for £1,000. The ducal bones were removed to Framlingham church in Suffolk, and the grand church of St. Mary of Thetford speedily went into decay. ⌐

---

1 Readers of Chaucer will know that 'womb' in Middle English could describe all of the stomach region. Matthew Paris' words can be translated as 'a crazy priest whose belly is like a bottle,' or 'a drunken clerical psychopath.'
2 The holy hoard included: the robe of Jesus, the girdle of Our Lady, a piece of the manger, a rock of Calvary and the grave clothes of Lazarus.

News travelled slowly in the sixteenth century and pilgrims continued to arrive for months after the priory had been closed and the monks dispersed.

There are still substantial ruins of the priory to be seen but the most intact is the impressive gatehouse built in the mid-fourteenth century and probably paid for by the pilgrims. It is built of cut flint and stone dressings. The principal accommodation was on the first floor and must have been very comfortable for the time, with fireplaces and a vaulted privy in one of the turrets. To one side was a barn which remained until the nineteenth century. Restoration work in the twentieth century replaced the tops of the turrets and parapet but not the crenellations.

13 LYCH GATE, KILVERSTONE

THE LYCH GATES OF NORFOLK'S CHURCHYARDS are the most significant portals in the county, witness to countless weddings and funerals. Their purpose in medieval times is suggested by the word, 'lych', Old English for corpse. At funerals the body rested at the gate before processing to the church. Besides this functional role, a lych gate is the formal and symbolic portal to the consecrated ground of the churchyard. This fine arts and crafts specimen stands at the entrance to the churchyard at Kilverstone. It has an added distinction, apart from its accomplished and unusual design, for here one of the most powerful and unusual men of twentieth century Britain passed on his way to church. When you stand beneath the oak-framed roof you are in the footsteps of Admiral of the Fleet Lord 'Jacky' Fisher, the endlessly fascinating and controversial First Sea Lord who modernised and reformed the Royal Navy before the first world war and created the Grand Fleet that fought the world's greatest naval battle at Jutland in 1916.

Fisher's connection with Kilverstone began when he was invited to shoot on the estate by its owner Josiah Vavasseur, the technical director of Armstrong, Whitworth & Company, the greatest armaments manufacturer in the world. Vavasseur had bought Kilverstone Hall with its 3,000 acre estate in 1900 and commissioned Norwich architect Edward Boardman[1] to remodel the existing house which dated from 1620. Boardman added new wings, extensive outbuildings and a very tall and rather sinister looking water tower.[2]

In 1908 Vavasseur died childless and left the hall and estate to Fisher's son Cecil on the condition that he took Vavasseur as his middle name. Jacky Fisher came to live there in 1910 when he retired as First Sea Lord and his aggressive crest of a mailed fist brandishing a trident was added to the gateposts.

Despite his ruthlessness and 3-H motto: HIT FIRST! HIT HARD! and KEEP ON HITTING![3] Fisher was an enthusiastic churchman who loved a good sermon and theological wrangle. We can imagine him bombarding the rector in the lych gate with broadsides of Biblical texts while the poor man was anxious to get home to lunch.

When he died in 1920 Fisher was buried in the quiet churchyard where he lies beneath a simple headstone on the north side. His grave is very neglected now, covered in lichen and almost illegible, which is rather ironic for a man whose handwriting was so forceful it scored the paper. You can only just read the description of his crowning achievement in his typically eccentric typography: 'Organizer of the Navy that WON the Great War.'

A 6-inch gun on a Vavasseur mounting. The gun recoiled, controlled by a hydraulic cylinder, up the inclined plane of the carriage. It was this invention that made Vavasseur's fortune.

---

1 Edward Boardman (1833–1910) was the most prolific Norwich architect of the second half of the nineteenth century, able to work in a variety of styles. The old Norfolk and Norwich Hospital and the former Royal Hotel are but two of his major works. George Skipper was his only serious rival.
2 This was built in 1905 a little before Skipper built the great campanile water tower at Sennowe Park. It is probably not a coincidence that the latter is taller than Kilverstone's.
3 He also made the uncomfortable but true point: 'The essence of war is violence. Moderation in war is imbecility.'

Lord Fisher, anxious to correct an inaccurate Biblical quotation and to continue the theological argument, pursues the rector.

Vavasseur gave generously to charities and paid to have the church of St Andrew restored by Boardman, who also designed the lych gate. The date, 1907, is marked by flints set in the floor. The gate is octagonal with a crisp stone and flint base supporting a sturdy oak frame finely carved with vines and sixteen charming squirrels eating acorns. The tiled roof with ingenious and elegant framing is a miniature broached spire with dormers. Over a century later, trees have grown up behind the gate, the oak has weathered to a subtle silver grey, the tiles are covered in moss, the astrolabe on the spire is broken and a thick electric cable has been carelessly tacked to one of the posts.

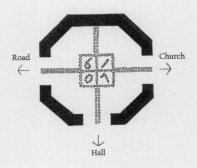

— 33 —

14 THE GREAT SIGN OF SCOLE INN

IN THE SEVENTEENTH AND EIGHTEENTH CENTURIES Scole was famous for the enormous and extravagant sign of the White Hart Inn that straddled the road like a proscenium arch. In an age when inn and shop signs displayed remarkable beauty and ingenuity, the Scole sign was a prodigy, famous throughout the land for its size and expense. It was enormous, spectacular and vulgar.

Up to forty coaches a day passed through Scole. In 1655, to take advantage of this trade, a Norwich wool merchant, John Peck, built the inn, one of the first with the specific purpose of entertaining travellers, to provide lodgings and fresh coach horses and to take post office deliveries. With a shrewd grasp of publicity, he gave additional distinction to the accommodation by providing a vast circular bed that could sleep thirty people.[1]

The wonder of the sign was the mass of carving that populated it with mythological figures and a menagerie of animals. An extraordinary cast of twenty-nine figures and twenty-one animals included Diana, Father Time, a whale and Cerberus, the terrible three-

headed guard dog of hell clawing at the support post. The most ingenious feature was a small figure sitting on a brass surveyor's compass that turned to face the direction of the rain. The sheer lavishness of the sign and the wealth of allegorical references in the figures contrasted sharply with the austerity of the times. England was then ruled by Cromwell's major-generals who busied themselves with chopping down maypoles and banning Christmas. The swaggering ostentation of the sign and especially its motto, *Implentur veteris bacchi pinguisquae ferinae*,[2] was surely an elaborate riposte to the puritans and their grim godliness.

The sign was made by John Fairchild and cost the vast sum of £1,057 – the inn itself cost only £1,500. It certainly fulfilled Peck's hopes of notoriety, for there was scarcely anyone in England who had not heard of it by the end of the century. But fame did not bring fortune. There was insufficient trade and the inn, despite being patronised by Charles II, did not prosper. Peck's hopes that it would become a venue for balls, concerts and assemblies came to nothing.

The sign stood, overawing all who passed beneath, until the 1750s when it was taken down, not because it was unsafe but because its baroque exuberance offended the more refined taste of the Georgians. They regarded it not as a triumph of good taste, but as a 'prodigy of human folly' and 'a sign of insanity', exciting the vacant wonder of only shallow intellects. M.J. Armstrong, writing in 1781, sneered, 'What could induce a merchant... to erect such a costly piece of workmanship, we are at a loss to conjecture, for we do not discover the smallest trait of judgement or taste in the whole composition. Had he (Peck) consulted every artist in the kingdom to leave a monument to his stupidity, they could not have produced a better effect.'

---

1 The Great Bed of Ware was made in 1590. 13 feet wide it could accommodate at least four couples.
   It is mentioned in Shakespeare's *Twelfth Night* and is now in the Victoria and Albert Museum.
2 Filled with vintage wine and fat game.

Charles II, not used to being ignored, is disconcerted to find that his subjects are more fascinated by the carved figures on the sign than his regal presence.

1 Jonah and the whale **2** Bacchus **3** Shepherds piping **4** The white hart with a motto **5** Neptune on a dolphin **6** Charon carrying a witch to hell **7** Cerberus **8** A huntsman **9** Acteon **10** Prudence **11** Fortitude **12** Temperance **13** Justice **14** Diana **15** Time devouring an infant **16** An astronomer seated on a surveyor's compass

Doubts have been expressed that this prodigy was ever built. The first printed sources that mention the sign date from the late eighteenth century when it had supposedly been demolished. Daniel Defoe passed by on his tour of the Eastern Counties and ignored it, which seems odd if such a wonder actually existed. It is surprising that there are no surviving fragments and that not a single piece of all that elaborate statuary was preserved. Arthur Mee claims there are fragments in the Victoria and Albert Museum but enquiries have proved this to be false.

15 BRITANNIA BARRACKS

IN 1881 LONG OVERDUE REFORMS were made to the British Army. The most important of these was to base each of the regiments in a county from where it would recruit. The 9th regiment of foot became the Norfolk Regiment. The obvious place for it to be based was Norwich but there were no suitable barracks. Those in Nelson Street were too small and old and the War Office intended to close them.

The city protested, and pleaded for a home for the new regiment. The War Office agreed to build a brand new barracks on the condition that Norwich provided the land. In 1884 a public subscription was opened by the Mayor, Sir Peter Eade,[1] and £1,600 was quickly raised. Land on Mousehold Heath was bought from the Church Commissioners and work began in 1886.

Because the site was so prominent the city insisted that the barracks must be of a pleasing appearance: an architectural ornament and not an eyesore. The architects were not from the Office of Works or the Royal Engineers, as was usually the case for barracks, but the private partnership of Kirk Randall and R.Lawrence Scott.[2]

Their design satisfied the council with a dramatic facade in a vaguely Scottish Baronial, Arts and Crafts style. 'A lonely piece of theatre isolated on the Mousehold Hills.' The architectural historian Nikolaus Pevsner finds this surprising as barracks were usually surrounded by grim walls adorned with faux medieval details. It was called the Britannia Barracks after the emblem of Britannia on the regimental badge.

The main range overlooking the city contained the officers' mess, administration offices and the armoury, housed in a solid keep with battered walls and slit windows. Behind was the parade ground and, as they were not on public view, four utilitarian barrack blocks and various buildings for training. There was accommodation for 440 officers and men, rather less than the full complement of a battalion of 800. This was because the new regiments had two battalions. One at full strength would normally be serving somewhere in the Empire; the second, back in barracks, trained new recruits and sent them out to the first.

From 1888 until 1959 tens of thousands of men passed through the gate to begin their service in the Norfolks. So many wanted to join in the early days of the first world war that 1,600 men camped on the heath as there was no room for them in the barracks. During the second world war it was just as busy, with the added danger of attack from the air. Although figuring on the Luftwaffe's meticulous target maps the barracks were bombed only twice; incendiary bombs fell on the barrack square and a small bomb exploded outside the gate, damaging the sentry box but not the sentry.

In 1959 the Royal Norfolk Regiment was amalgamated with the Suffolk Regiment. The barracks were redundant and considered as a site for the UEA. Empty for some years they were bought by the Home Office in 1971 and absorbed into the prison. The old officers' mess was for many years the staff social club but is now a cafe, open to the public and staffed by the prisoners.

---

1 Eade was consultant surgeon at the Norfolk & Norwich Hospital and was three times mayor of Norwich. It was largely owing to his efforts that Chapel Field Gardens were laid out and Mousehold Heath developed as a park.
2 One wonders why local architects like Skipper and Boardman were not considered.

'It has been decreed in several line battalions (including the Norfolk Regiment) that in future no soldier will be allowed to walk arm-in-arm in the streets with a female.'

The gate had no defensive purpose but made a suitably martial entrance to what could easily have passed as a block of mansion flats or a college for young ladies. It is built of red brick with masonry dressing and ornamental details in the local decorative terracotta known as Cosseyware. There are several ritual loopholes and the battered walls give an aspect of stern determination. The large keep-like building to the right was the armoury and the guardroom was to the left, including the small tower which vaguely suggests the bartizans or sentry posts on seventeenth century fortifications.

16 NORWICH CITY GAOL

FOR SEVERAL CENTURIES Norwich had two prisons. This was because the city had its own magistrates as well as being the county town of Norfolk and the seat of the assizes for the King's judges. Those convicted by the magistrates were imprisoned in the city's prison and those by the assizes were held in the county prison in the ancient castle. The city prison was on Gaol Hill by the Guildhall. It was cramped and very unhealthy and in 1822 the magistrates resolved to build a new model prison on an open air site just outside the city walls at the junction of Earlham and, what is now, Unthank Roads. An original design by the eminent engineer William Cubitt was rejected and that of a Norwich architect, Philip Barnes, chosen instead. Work began on the new gaol in 1824 and was completed in 1827 to general satisfaction.

It was a handsome, if austere building, completely symmetrical in plan, surrounded by a wall 23 feet high. There were four two-storey wings, two for felons and two for debtors, with 114 cells, eight day rooms, an infirmary and eight exercise yards. At the centre was the three-storied governor's house with an inspection gallery – modelled on Jeremy Bentham's Panopticon – from where he could overlook the exercise yards. To keep the prisoners from idleness there were three large treadmills[1] which pumped water from the well. The cost of the building was £30,000 and there were usually about seventy prisoners and a dozen debtors in residence. The staff was small: only eight, including the governor with a visiting chaplain, surgeon and schoolmaster.

In 1881 the national system was reorganised, abolishing the need for two separate prisons. The castle prison was bought by the corporation of Norwich, who transformed it into the museum and gallery we know today. The city gaol was sold to the Duke of Norfolk, who had resolved to provide the local Roman Catholics with a new church. Before the old gaol was demolished in 1881 the parish priest admitted the public, who were curious to see what lay behind the grim facade, at sixpence (2.5p) a head. Work on St John's Church – it was made a cathedral only in 1976 – was delayed for two years while old chalk workings were filled in to prepare the foundations. A new prison was built on Mousehold Heath behind the Britannia Barracks, where it still functions.

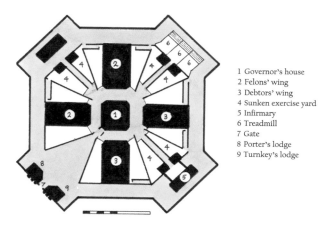

1 Governor's house
2 Felons' wing
3 Debtors' wing
4 Sunken exercise yard
5 Infirmary
6 Treadmill
7 Gate
8 Porter's lodge
9 Turnkey's lodge

1 The treadmill was invented by William Cubitt in 1818. It looked like a paddle wheel with a cylinder of twenty-four steps, placed at a distance of one foot and a half from each other. It rotated in a uniform motion and compelled prisoners to walk side by side and to ascend a never-ending staircase by stepping on the paddle's blades. Cubitt thought of the idea when he saw idle prisoners at Bury St Edmund's gaol.

Mr Phillip Barnes shows the magistrates, with the aid of the turnkey's wife, how a statue of Justice would be a fitting adornment to the gaol's principal gate. He was overruled on grounds of economy.

The massive gateway expressed the intimidating function of the prison behind with grim elegance. It was built of Yorkshire stone and, with its muscular rustication and stout Tuscan columns, owed much to Dance's design for London's Newgate Prison. In the niches were fasces: an axe bound with rods, the Roman symbol of justice and punishment. Above in panels were swags of manacles and leg irons, just in case in anyone should fail to realise the purpose of the building. The gate occupied the site of the east end of the Catholic cathedral facing the end of the footbridge across Grape's Hill. The site of the treadmills is in the garden by the Narthex cafe.

17 THE BISHOP'S GATE, NORWICH

 NORWICH CATHEDRAL AND PRIORY were enclosed by a tall, strong wall to give protection to the monks from an often hostile city and to mark the separation of the two communities, which had different laws and privileges. Much of it, along with four of the six gates, still remains.

The Bishop's Gate, opposite St Martin's church, is the entrance to the Bishop's Palace. It was begun in about 1430 by Bishop Alnwick and was completed by his successor, Bishop Lyhart. The gate served its defensive purpose keeping out Kett's rebels, who surged about the doors during the fight of 1st August 1549, but that was the last time it was attacked. Afterwards it was nothing more than a grand front door. Numerous notable clerics have passed beneath its arch but the most famous visitor was Queen Elizabeth who stayed in the Bishop's Palace during her only visit to Norwich in 1578.

The city contrived many unusual ways to honour the Queen, making each prolonged speech of welcome – there were six on the first day – into a costumed pageant. After such a surfeit of speechifying the Queen spent all of Sunday secluded in the Bishop's Palace. But early on Monday she was surprised by a gilded coach rumbling up to the gate with a fanfare of trumpets. The horses were fitted with wings ingeniously made of paper and feathers, and their hides were painted to match the coach. A boy dressed as Mercury jumped out and treated the surprised Queen to an elegant speech in Latin. This was not the last oration Elizabeth had to endure during her five-day visit. Finally, her patience exhausted, she stopped the Mayor from speaking and demanded his manuscript instead.

The coach and its winged steeds was the most bizarre vehicle to arrive at the gate, although the first motor cars looked very peculiar and, at some time in the nineteenth century, there must have been a clergyman who arrived to see the bishop on a penny-farthing bicycle.

In 1975 Bishop Maurice Woods[1] launched a campaign of evangelisation for rural Norfolk. He bought thirty-six Honda mopeds at a bargain price and issued them to a selected band of clergy. The bishop blessed them and their vehicles from the steps of his house[2] before the convoy of crash-helmeted, dog-collared clerics putt-putted through the gate to go forth and spread the gospel. The campaign was not a success as most of the clergy sensibly preferred cars and there was something inescapably comic about a vicar on a moped, wearing cycle clips and a crash helmet with earflaps.

---

1 Bishop of Norwich from 1971 to 1985. He was a leader of the evangelical wing of the Church of England, at odds with his fellow bishops over his theological and political positions.
2 The grand Bishop's Palace had been taken over by the Norwich School in 1958 and the bishop had moved to a new and more manageable new house built just inside the gate.

Mercury arrives to amaze and amuse Queen Elizabeth I.

The Bishop's Gate is a fine example of a perpendicular gateway and much simpler than the two gates facing Tombland. It is built of flint with stone dressing and there are two polygonal turrets on the inside. There are two arches, the larger for carriages and the smaller for pedestrians. The archway is vaulted with a carved boss and the doors are the original fifteenth century ones. Carved in the door of the pedestrian entrance is Bishop Lyhart's rebus – a heart lying on its side. Apart from the restored battlements, which are largely ornamental, the gate has no defensive features such as loopholes and relied only on the strength of the doors to keep out attackers.

18 THE ERPINGHAM GATE, NORWICH

IT IS RATHER IRONIC but quite typical that a splendid ornament to religion should have been financed from a fortune accrued in bloody warfare. The Erpingham Gate of the Cathedral Close, through which, before the Reformation, passed religious processions and cavalcades of devout pilgrims, was built on the proceeds of the Hundred Years War. It was paid for by Sir Thomas Erpingham, staunch retainer of Henry IV and commander of the archers at the battle of Agincourt.[1] He made a fortune through his position at court and his share of the ransoms of captured French nobles. Like many an elderly warrior in those times he prudently resolved to spend a portion of his dubiously gained wealth on adorning the cause of religion.[2]

The gate was built between 1420 and 1425, replacing a more modest, utilitarian structure. After the Reformation the religious ceremonies ceased and were replaced by civic and legal processions arriving to give thanks in the cathedral. The grandest of these was the Guild Day, a pageant to inaugurate the election of a new mayor.[3] The procession, regarded to be the finest civic cavalcade in England, began at the new mayor's house and passed through the city to enter The Close at the Erpingham Gate. First came the snap dragon, guarded by four swordsmen or whifflers. Next followed the city beadles with a band and the city's great standard, followed by the common council in gowns, with their beadle, and the city coroners. After them came the city waits, singing merrily, the standard of justice, a magnificent array of macebearers, swordbearers, chamberlains, recorders, sheriffs, stewards (high and low), aldermen and the mayor and mayor elect.

Arriving at the cathedral three knocks were given before the doors opened and the procession walked on rushes to the choir. A service was sung and they endured an interminable, but doubtless edifying, sermon preached by the mayor's chaplain. Before they could leave The Close they were treated to a Latin oration, specially composed, delivered by the head scholar of the Grammar School. The procession then returned to the Guildhall, where the new mayor was invested and there were yet more speeches addressed to the old and new mayors. Then, at last, they adjourned to St. Andrew's Hall for a splendid banquet, to which every distinguished person in the city and neighbourhood was invited.

The Municipal Act of 1835 reformed the city's government on more democratic lines and the opulent festivities were discontinued. But the Erpingham Gate still sees the arrival of the judges for the annual Judges Service and the Lord Mayor in his coach for the Civic Service.

---

1 His role in the battle was famous enough to be remembered by Shakespeare, who celebrates him as 'the good old knight' in *Henry V*.

2 Another story is that Sir Thomas built the gate as a penance for having espoused the cause of the heretic Wycliffe. The bishop had him arrested and committed to prison, compelling him to erect the gate as a condition of release.

3 The event originated in the annual procession of St. George's Guild and was kept up when that body was dissolved at the Reformation.

4 Thought to mean either think or thank. Maybe it's not a 'Y' but a Þ (thorn) routinely mistaken for 'Y' as in 'ye olde...'

Snap, the civic dragon, leads the Guild Day procession through the gate into The Close.

The arch is populated by thirty-eight statues of men and women, including Sir Thomas's two wives. The semi-octangular buttresses are divided into four compartments, covered with statues, niches, shields, and pedestals. The carving includes trees, birds, and several scrolls with the cryptic word Yenk.[4] In a canopied niche in the pediment is a kneeling statue, supposedly of Sir Thomas. The niche was empty until the eighteenth century and the statue is thought to have come from Sir Thomas's tomb in the cathedral which explains why he seems uncomfortably cramped in the space and his expression less than serene.

19 ST ETHELBERT'S GATE, NORWICH

THE NAME TOMBLAND[1] suggests the calm of a cemetery but it has always been a lively place. Busy with traffic by day and raucous revellers by night it continues the rumbustious traditions of the Middle Ages when an annual, and often unruly, fair was held there. The fair of 1272 ended in even greater violence than usual. Relations between the city and the cathedral priory had never been good, with disputes over rights and boundaries. Hostility came to a head at the fair when the citizens erected a quintain[2] in a spot deliberately chosen to annoy the monks. A fight began with servants of the priory, who killed a citizen.

The city coroners arrested two servants, and the prior retaliated by excommunicating the citizens. After a month the priory was besieged, with the gates closed and mercenary soldiers firing at the citizens with a giant crossbow from the top of the belfry inside the walls. After peace negotiations broke down, the prior brought in more mercenaries from Yarmouth. These attacked the city at night, killing one man, wounding others, looting and setting fire to houses.

A mob of enraged citizens stormed the priory, destroying a gate and the small church beside it. They set fire to the cathedral and adjacent buildings and indulged in an orgy of retaliatory looting that lasted three days. The monks fled but some clerics and servants were killed and others dragged off into the city. However, it was not all one-sided; the prior killed one of the attackers himself.

The affair was so unsettling that King Henry III sent a commission to pacify the city and then came to personally supervise the investigation. A selection of rioters were tried and twenty-nine hanged. A further investigation blamed the priory's violence and with this sharing of blame the affair was settled in 1275. The city was fined, made to pay damages to the priory and to beg pardon of the pope. The priory had to build a new gate to The Close, incorporating a chapel on its upper floor. This new gate was called St Ethelbert's after the destroyed church and was completed in about 1325.

The chapel was disused by 1500 and later was converted to a concert room in association with the adjoining tavern. In the twentieth century it served as the art room for the Norwich School. Today there is a rest room for The Close gatekeepers on the ground floor; the upper chamber is used as a music room and filled with drum kits.

---

1 From the Old English *tom* meaning empty. So empty space or open ground.
2 A quintain was a device used in jousting games. It consisted of a tall pole with a beam across the top. One end of the beam was widened into a target; from the other a bag of sand or bucket of water was suspended. The aim was to strike the target squarely with a lance. If the blow was a poor one or the lance missed, the beam swung round and the bag hit the player or the bucket drenched him.

In the bleak midwinter of 1962 Bishop Lancelot Fleming (1959–1971) leads the cathedral choir through St Ethelbert's Gate to bring Christmas cheer to the city's shivering shoppers. The sub-zero temperatures held no terrors for the intrepid bishop; he had been awarded the Scott Polar Medal for his service as chaplain to the British Antarctic Expedition.

The gate uses the shell of the one destroyed in the riot. The elaborate facade with its magnificent three rose windows in flint flushwork is a very early, if not the first, use of this technique. The roses are not quite the originals as William Wilkins heavily restored the gate in 1815 and altered the pattern. Most of the stonework and the carving of a man drawing a sword against a dragon – perhaps a not too subtle allusion to the events of 1272 – were restored in 1965. Inside the passage there is a two-bayed lierne vault with a Green Man staring down from the carved boss.

20 SOUTH GATE, CAISTOR ST EDMUND

THE REMAINS OF VENTA ICENORUM (the Town of the Iceni) stand beside the River Tas at Caistor St Edmund, five miles south of Norwich. It was the largest town in Roman Norfolk, not that that was much to boast about, and gave an inkling of the possibilities of urban sophistication to the surrounding tribesfolk.

It was founded and laid out on the typical Roman grid plan in the last part of the first century. After the defeat of Boudicca's revolt the Romans chose the site to provide an administrative centre for the Iceni tribe. If a Roman from the great cities of the Empire found his way to this provincial backwater he would have found all the familiar urban elements, but on a very small scale. There was a basilica (the town hall and law courts), a forum, a market place, public baths and a supply of running water brought by an aqueduct from the high ground to the east. There was even a small amphitheatre outside the town and one can imagine third-rate gladiator troupes arriving to entertain the citizens, who had never seen anything better.[1] The aim of the Romans in founding such towns was to pacify the tribes and gradually introduce them to Roman customs. The richer Iceni took to a more Romanised way of life; Roman dress and habits like going to the baths and giving dinner parties became fashionable. A few would have learnt Latin and others would have practised trades and skills previously unknown.

There would have been very few, if any, actual Romans in the town. It had its own local council, presided over by two magistrates who were drawn from the leading local families. There is no record of a Roman official bemoaning his fate in being sent to such distant backwater.

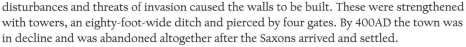

The town was at its most prosperous and peaceful up to about 250AD when civil disturbances and threats of invasion caused the walls to be built. These were strengthened with towers, an eighty-foot-wide ditch and pierced by four gates. By 400AD the town was in decline and was abandoned altogether after the Saxons arrived and settled.

When urban life revived in England it was Norwich that became the principal city of East Anglia and Venta was forgotten. Gradually the walls were robbed of their stone, which went to build Norwich. The antiquarians of the eighteenth century thought the remains were those of a Roman camp and it was not until a pilot flying overhead in 1928 noticed the grid of the streets plainly displayed in crop markings and realised it was actually a town. Subsequent excavations have revealed much of interest but nothing spectacular: Venta was always very small and probably very dull. 🏛

---

1 It is not fanciful to speculate that gladiators might have fought at Venta. A heavy bronze gladiator's helmet was found in 1965 at Hawkedon, near Lavenham which strongly supports the theory that there were gladiatorial games in Britain.

A gladiator wearing a helmet similar to that found at Hawkedon sets out for an evening appearance in the arena.

The South Gate was excavated in 1934 by Professor Donald Atkinson who found a 13 feet wide gate flanked, not by towers, but by the curving ends of the wall built of flints bonded with layers of thin Roman bricks. There was a chamber or possibly a tower above the gate, two square guardrooms on each side and a wooden bridge to cross the dry moat. Socket holes in the masonry suggest there were double doors. After the excavation was complete the remains were reburied so there is now nothing to see except a gap in the line of the wall. The walls were built of flints bonded with layers of thin Roman bricks.

21 THE WESTWICK ARCH

 THE WESTWICK ARCH on the road between Coltishall and North Walsham was a celebrated folly that delighted and infuriated motorists in equal measure until it was destroyed in 1981. The Arch and two flanking lodges were originally built in 1765 to form a grand entrance to the park of Westwick House. In 1794 the North Walsham Turnpike Trust straightened and shortened the road, which had followed the park boundary, by diverting it through the Arch, which then became the most impressive tollgate in the county.

When carts and carriages were horse-drawn the Arch was no impediment to traffic; nor was it when the first cars appeared and it was marked on motoring maps as a picturesque landmark, not a hazard. Before the first world war there were very few cars in North Norfolk and motoring was a pleasure reserved for the rich. Lady Battersea of *The Pleasuance* in Overstrand was a keen motorist (in the sense of being driven rather than driving) who welcomed the car's extension of her social radius and often visited the Petre family at Westwick House.

In 1906 The Ladies Automobile Club[1] made a tour of Norfolk and passed beneath the Arch. The small convoy of exotic motor vehicles[2] and their aristocratic drivers included the Countess of Kinnoull, 'one of the very beautiful members of the Club and an ardent and accomplished all-weather motorist', and Lady Margaret Jenkins, who despite having 'adopted automobilism *con amore*', only steered her car. Operating the gear lever, brake and accelerator was far too taxing.[3]

This motoring idyll did not last long and, as traffic on the road grew inexorably heavier and vehicles larger, the Arch was increasingly regarded as an impediment and not an adornment. It survived being hit by buses, lorries and numerous cars until August 1981. A survey then revealed that the Arch was cracked and in such a bad state that the road was immediately closed. Repairs were estimated at £30,000; the county council offered £5,000. This was not enough for the owners, the Westwick Estate, who demolished the Arch with great alacrity on the very day it was made a Grade 2 listed monument. They claimed no knowledge of the decision and protested that there was no option. The council, anxious to reopen the road, accepted what had been done and took the opportunity to widen the carriageway. The two lodges escaped destruction and still remain.

---

1 The Ladies' Automobile Club had been founded in 1903 when the RAC refused to admit women. Their clubhouse was part of Claridges Hotel, chosen to simplify the pressing problem of feminine life, 'How to cope with the Modern Servant'.
2 The cars included a Carron-Girardot & Voight, a Chenard & Walcker, a Nesseldorfer, a steam-powered Vapomobile and a racing Darracq.
3 She refused to go more than twenty miles an hour, protesting that such a high speed not only destroyed every vestige of a woman's beauty but spoilt the artistic appreciation of the scenery and the many points of roadside picturesqueness, of which the Westwick Arch was a notable example.

Lady Cecil Scott Montagu, accompanied by the society milliner Lady Rachel Byng, who constructed the dust proof hats, drives her 12 h.p. Wolseley through the Arch.

The Arch was built of red brick rendered over with cement. The heavily rusticated quoins on the south face were made of flint pebbles – those on the north face of knapped flint. The little pointed holes in gothic niches on either side indicate that the arch had been used as a dovecote. The pediment and its simple but dignified mouldings were of wood, presumably to make the structure lighter and cheaper. The road was 18 feet wide under the arch which was ample room for most vehicles although double-decker buses took the middle of the carriageway.

22 NORTH GATE, GREAT YARMOUTH

 THE TOWN WALL OF GREAT YARMOUTH is its greatest hidden treasure. Behind the ugly bulk of the Market Gates Centre, in back gardens, overlooking dreary car parks and tired playgrounds, are some of the most extensive and impressive remains of medieval fortifications in England. Only Chester and York have more complete circuits than Yarmouth.

Built between 1276 and 1390, the wall was one and a quarter miles long – of which two thirds remain – with sixteen towers, two principal and seven smaller gates. 23 feet high, it was built of flint, with bonding courses of brick, topped with expensive Caen Stone battlements. The upper stories of the towers were rendered in a striking chequered pattern of alternating squares of knapped flint and smooth plaster. The rampart walk was supported on arches, with a loophole in the wall of each recess.

During the sixteenth century the walls were adapted to meet the threat of artillery. Earth was heaped up behind the wall to make a rampart 40 feet thick.[1] Arches were built at the back of the gates to make the path along the ramparts continuous and this proved popular as a promenade. In 1569 a huge earth mound – the East Mount – was raised, where St George's church now stands, on which eight guns were mounted to command the beach and the anchorage of Yarmouth Roads. During the Armada scare of 1588 a brick-faced bastion[2] was built in front of the East Mount and earthwork bastions placed in advance of the South Gate. Between the South Gate and the river another mound – the South Mount – was raised and guns emplaced upon it to cover the river and Denes. These soon decayed but were repaired and remodelled during the Civil War when Yarmouth declared for Parliament. A new ditch was dug and an earth rampart with five bastions raised before the North Gate, extending round the north-east corner of the medieval walls. These additions made Yarmouth a powerful and modern fortress. After the war the fortifications were allowed to decay and were hidden or obliterated by new buildings.

The North Gate was the main entrance to the town where the road from Norwich and north-east Norfolk entered. It was a very handsome structure as befitting the entrance to a proud and prosperous town. It was completed in about 1360 and legend asserts that it was paid for by those who became rich burying the dead during the Black Death.

The gate was demolished in 1807 as an obstruction to traffic but its position is quite plain from the section of surviving town wall to the east of the road.

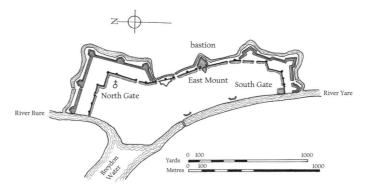

The fortifications of Yarmouth at their greatest extent in 1645.

---

1 This can still be seen behind the stretch of wall along Blackfriars Road.
2 This is partially buried beneath Ravelin House but the salient with curved brick parapet and stone cordon can still be seen from St Peter's Plain.

An eighteenth century tourist takes a ride in a Yarmouth Coach, the passenger version of the unique Troll Cart that had evolved to travel through the narrow rows. Painted in bright colours, the coaches proved popular with visitors, although upsets were common.

The gatehouse was 60 feet wide and the arch 12 feet wide, closed by two sets of doors and a portcullis. Two square towers with corner buttresses of dressed flint and Caen stone flanked the arch, surmounted by a machicolated parapet. Beneath this were decorated panels consisting of an arcade of stone lancets filled with flint. Despite its imposing appearance it was not a very effective fortification. The buttresses made flanking the faces of the tower impossible and there are only two loopholes, although the two small round holes beneath the parapet may have been for handguns.

23 LACON'S BREWERY, GREAT YARMOUTH

LACON'S BREWERY STOOD on Fuller's Hill from the mid-eighteenth century to 1968 where it brewed countless convivial kegs of festive ale. Founded in 1764 by Mr Edward Laycon (the Y was soon dropped) the original small brewhouse expanded relentlessly to eventually occupy most of the space between Fuller's Hill and The Conge. The tall brewing tower, viewed from the Acle Road, soared above the town like a campanile, rivalling the spire of the parish church. In 1814 Lacon's provided 70 barrels of ale (or 20,000 pints) to lubricate the celebrations of the first defeat of Napoleon, at a great dinner for 8,000 people seated all along the South Quay. By 1845 Lacons were sending beer to London and owned over fifty pubs in Yarmouth and the surrounding villages.

In 1868 a railway siding was built into the brewery to speed up deliveries to London where Lacon's had many tied houses.[1] Sir Edmund Lacon had been an enthusiastic supporter of railways and was one of the original promoters of the Yarmouth & Norwich Railway, which opened in 1844.

The company's success enriched and ennobled the family; Edmund Lacon was created the first Baron Lacon in 1818 and his son Sir Edmund Henry Knowles Lacon became member of parliament for Yarmouth, a prominent Liberal politician, Deputy Lieutenant of Norfolk and commander of the infamous Yarmouth artillery volunteers, who so often disgraced themselves by an over liberal use of his product. He was also, rather ironically, the chairman of the Great Yarmouth Water Company.

In 1942 there was a heavy air raid on Yarmouth and thousands of incendiaries showered down. The brewery and St Nicolas's church were set ablaze and an overstretched fire brigade had to decide which source of comfort to save. They chose beer and the church was gutted.

In 1952 the Lacons family floated the company on the stock exchange and the process of it ceasing to be a family firm began. In 1957 Whitbread bought 20 percent of the stock and in 1965 took complete control. It was hardly a surprise three years later when the brewery was closed and demolished, apart from the bottle store which survived until 1997, when it was sacrificed for a supermarket. All seemed lost until 2013 when the name was revived and a new firm began brewing under the old name, but not on the original site.

---

1 At its zenith the company had 354 public houses: fifty in London and a remarkable 176 in Yarmouth. They were usually distinguished by a falcon on a ceramic plaque and architectural detailing using thin Roman bricks.

The Great Yarmouth Crusade Against Intoxicating Liquor makes its annual demonstration at the gate in 1956.

The famous and elaborate gate was built in 1865 in a typically Victorian eclectic style of brick with stone and terracotta dressings. The main element was a variety of baroque but with hints of Jacobean. The famous Lacon's falcon perched high above the arch and the initials of Edmund Henry Knowles Lacon adorned the shield. The horse chestnut tree in the courtyard added a graceful rural aspect to the scene. When Whitbread took over Lacons in 1965 they quickly closed and demolished the brewery. No effort was made to spare this splendid gate and incorporate it in the dull and ugly buildings that have replaced the brewery.

24 WELLINGTON ARCHES, GREAT YARMOUTH

 IN THE 1830S THERE WAS A GROWING DEMAND for sea bathing and the healthy benefits of the seaside and Yarmouth had spread outside its medieval walls towards the beach. Some local businessmen considered this new and meanly built part of the town impossible to improve and decided to create a new suburb that would be another Brighton or a seaside version of Belgravia.

In July 1841 the Victoria Building Company was formed,[1] with the intention of making Great Yarmouth an attractive resort for the reception of 'families of the highest rank'. Land was bought on the South Denes between the Jetty and the South Battery,[2] deserted but for the Nelson Column, a naval hospital and a barracks for the militia. The company planned a spacious esplanade and elegant streets and squares. The new district was to be called, inevitably, Victoria.

The scheme, designed by Thomas Marsh, was vast, with magnificent crescents and imposing leafy squares with terraces of houses in three classes – grand, substantial and modest. The Company did not build the houses directly but leased plots with stipulations on how the buildings were to be constructed. The front elevation had to conform to the broad design laid out by the architect to maintain a uniform look to the streets. To dignify the entrance to this enclave of gentility there were to be two grand arches on the north side. No shops or public houses would be allowed within the estate, to maintain the high social tone and to mollify objections that trade would be taken from existing businesses. An elegant hotel called the Victoria (what else?) was one of the first buildings to be erected.[3]

Building proceeded slowly and by 1845 only Kimberley Terrace was complete. In 1846 the large entry arch was completed but its companion was never started. The smaller of the two arches we can see today was built the next year as the entrance to the mews behind the terrace.

Over the next decade the original ambitious scheme was trimmed; the grand crescents and Mr Mohamed's Medicated Vapour Baths never materialised. What stands today is little more than a tenth of the original conception.

It was a wasted opportunity to hide the arches away behind the grand sea front terraces, seen by only coachmen and domestics instead of being admired by the superior visitors taking the sea air on the new marine parade. But within a decade the gentry were greatly outnumbered by visitors of less refinement. After the railway was opened in 1844, at first to Norwich and then to London and the Midlands, the numbers of visitors of an inferior class soon greatly exceeded the superior ones the estate had been designed for. Walter Rye complained that it was only possible to admire 'the fine prospect of grand sands and excellent houses at 4.30am on a fine summer morning. Later than this throngs of cockneys begin to emerge from the numerous small lodging-houses and render the place unsavoury.'

---

1 It lasted until 1968 when it was finally wound up.
2 The Board of Ordnance was consulted and stipulated that the buildings should be so arranged as not to interfere with the field of fire of the South Battery's guns.
3 It is now the Carlton Hotel.

The soul of Dawson Turner, banker, botanist, art collector and trustee of the Victoria Building Company, returns in the form of a seagull to view the dismal fruition of his dream.

The larger of the two arches seen from behind the smaller.
Built in 1846 by John Brown of yellow gault brick with rendered details. The large plain semicircular arch with mouldings and a large keystone is flanked by two similar, smaller pedestrian arches. To right and left are plain giant pilasters rising to an entablature. A projecting cornice, with a simple balustrade at the top gives a dramatic aspect to the ensemble. In 1955 the Victoria Building Company petitioned the Ministry of Works to demolish both arches. Fortunately, at a time when the reputation of Victorian triumphal architecture was at its nadir, permission was refused. They were restored in 1980.

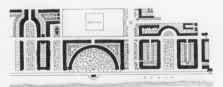

The great crescent and squares of the original plan never materialised. Only a small portion – in the bottom right corner – was ever built.

25 SOUTH GATE, GREAT YARMOUTH

THE SECOND PRINCIPAL GATE of Yarmouth was the South Gate, leading out on to what were, then sand dunes. Built in about 1320, it was an impressive structure combining both elements of display and defence. The gate was flanked by two towers and closed by strong doors and a portcullis. The upper stories of the towers were ornamented by a grid of rectangular panels, alternately filled with flush black flint and plaster.

The military history of the gate was uneventful and it was never seriously threatened, although it did deny Kett's rebels entry into the town before they destroyed the uncompleted works of the sixth haven.[1] During the Armada emergency and the Civil War a ditch and an earth rampart were thrown up before the gate but these were decayed and eroded by the mid-eighteenth century. The last time the gate was considered as an effective fortification was in 1793 when a report recommended repairing the walls and blocking the gates with heavy carts and wagons chained together.

Many travellers arriving by sea landed on the beach or at the jetty, from ships anchored in Yarmouth Roads, and the very important, worthy of a civic reception, made their entrance to the town through the South Gate. The most illustrious was King William III who made a triumphant progress through the gate after landing from his yacht anchored in the Roads.

There was more rejoicing on the 18th February, 1807 when Captain Manby[2] brought the crew of the brig *Elizabeth* into the town after their ship was wrecked off the beach. He had saved them from certain death with the first successful demonstration of his life-saving Manby Mortar.

Manby had been greatly moved by the loss of sixty-seven lives when HMS *Snipe* was wrecked off the south beach. Although within 50 yards of the shore and would-be rescuers, the crew drowned, for there was no way to reach them through the surf. Manby had the idea of using a small mortar to fire a line attached to a cannon ball from the shore to the stricken ship. When this was secured to the ship a boat could be hauled out and then back with the rescued crew. About sixty stations equipped with his apparatus were established and, before Manby died in 1854, he had the satisfaction of knowing he had saved more than 1,000 lives. Over a hundred of these were off the Yarmouth beaches.

The gate was pulled down in 1812 when there was a positive rage for demolition and the feeble protests of antiquarians were ignored. Part of the west side with a loophole and a portion of the portcullis groove survived until 1867 when it succumbed to a scheme to widen the road.

---

1 Yarmouth stands on a spit of sand which originally stretched as far south as Corton. Throughout the Middle Ages channels were dug through the spit to make an entrance to the harbour close to the town. They always silted up, making a new one necessary. The present harbour entrance is the seventh haven, made in 1584.

2 George William Manby (1765–1854) was not a naval officer but a militia captain who had been appointed master of the barracks in Yarmouth in 1803. He was an inveterate inventor – of unsinkable boats, fire extinguishers and more lethal whale harpoons – with an obsessive interest in Nelson.

Captain Manby proudly enters the South Gate with the survivors of the *Elizabeth*.

By the early nineteenth century the tower was dilapidated, partially obscured by buildings, and the moat before it had long been filled in. The structure on the west tower is a semaphore apparatus erected in 1801. It was the first of a chain of sixteen semaphore stations that ran from Yarmouth to the Admiralty in London. A dispatch from a ship anchoring in the Roads could be in the First Sea Lord's hands within a matter of minutes. The system was invented by Lord George Murray, Bishop of St David's, and used six octagonal shutters that flipped from vertical to horizontal to make the patterns that spelled the letters. The system was abandoned in 1816 at the end of the Napoleonic Wars.

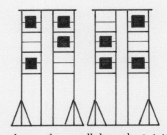

The shutters here spell the author's initials.

APPENDIX 1
✤ PRISON GATES ✤

PRISON GATES were always severe and strong, not so much to keep the prisoners in – high walls, locked doors and leg irons can easily do that – as to keep people out. A prison was as much a fortress to repel those bent on releasing the prisoners as a strong enclosure for containing them. As well as its practical purpose the prison gate had the powerful theatrical function to express the drama of crime and punishment. It was the point of transition from the free world to the confined.

52 Sir John Soane's County Gaol of 1793

The prisoner approached the stern gate and the doors swung open to admit him, closing behind with an implacable thud. On his release they opened again to a world of light into which he was permitted to return. Architects used either the classical or gothic style to emphasise this. Classical expressed a more rational approach to punishment; gothic had romantic suggestions of dungeons and dark memories of racks and thumbscrews. Both styles were grand, austere and overawing – no one designed a prison to be friendly and welcoming – and the gates of Norfolk's five principal gaols were suitably grim. The finest is that of King's Lynn Gaol built in 1784, its heavy rustication and decoration of chains derived from London's Newgate Prison. A new County Gaol beside Norwich castle was designed by Sir John Soane with a plain and elegant gothic gate, but soon replaced by a more aggressive mock fortification with turrets and machicolations. Norwich City Gaol was in a pure but stern classical style, while the current prison, opened in 1887, has a classic gate but with economically reduced details.

54 Norwich Prison of 1887

Norfolk's newest prison, Wayland, has an unassuming main entrance that could be a municipal office block with a loading bay door. This aptly expresses the shift in penal theory which has changed the prison from a place of retribution, whose aspect was intended to frighten, to a therapeutic asylum with appropriately unassertive architecture. 🏰

43 Wayland Prison

APPENDIX 2
✤ COUNTRY HOUSE GATES ✤

THE GREAT PARKS around country houses, mostly created in the eighteenth century, were the personal domain of the owner, devoted to his enjoyment and his alone. Often walled and always fenced, these domains demanded a significant entrance, one that proclaimed the magnificence of the house within and which also formed a frontier post on the border between the private and public worlds. The principal park gates invariably incorporated a lodge where the keepers lived to control entrance to the private kingdom.

46 Hanworth Lodge, Gunton

Architects in the eighteenth century always chose as their model the Roman triumphal arch which admirably served their purpose and usually matched the style of the great house. However, the romantic and gothic revival movements of the later eighteenth and nineteenth centuries saw large numbers of gates which looked like the battlemented entrances of

33 South Lodge, Hillingdon

castles. This was precisely the impression that the architect and his client were after. Gothic gates, as well as being fashionable, were also more flexible than the rigid template of the classical arch. The arch of the gate could be varied in its proportions of width to height and the keepers' lodge could be more easily incorporated into turrets and rooms over the arch. Later in the nineteenth century, as elaborate ironwork became cheaper, the arched gate gave way to ornamental metal gates, although the porters' lodge still remained a prominent feature.

The successors to the great gates of Holkham and Heydon are the elaborate gate pillars and useless stretches of adjoining wall found at the entrances of large, new and expensive houses. Here the ironwork is elaborate but invariably ugly and the porters have been replaced by an entry phone and surveillance camera. The twenty-first century equivalent of the porter's wife, bobbing a curtesy as a carriage full of gentry rolls by, is the electronic device that opens the gate in advance of the overlarge 4x4 with smoked windows.

APPENDIX 3

✠ ABBEY GATES ✠

IT IS OFTEN THOUGHT that the walls of monasteries were to keep the monks and nuns in but, instead, like prisons, they were to keep the world out. Mediaeval abbeys and priories were centres of agriculture and industry as well as being places of prayer and contemplation. They were full of valuable things. As such they were, like the great houses, the object of envy and, when law and order broke down, the prey of the covetous and the resentful. Religious scruples were no substitute for secular defences and every monastery had high walls and stout gates.

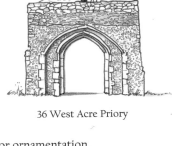

36 West Acre Priory

The walls were rarely crenellated or provided with towers, like a castle, but there was usually a gatehouse. Although imposing, these were never intended to be serious fortifications; their battlements were for ornamentation, the turrets for display. Few had loopholes and none had portcullises or drawbridges. They usually had accommodation for a porter and often rooms where rents were collected and a manorial court held. One of the functions of the gatehouse was to be the public office of the monastery and they mainly survive because these functions continued after the monastery was closed and turned to secular uses. Virtually all the gatehouses of the major monasteries in Norfolk have survived either as ruins, like the lonely remnants of St Benet's, or as functioning buildings like the gates to the Cathedral Close or Pentney Priory.

50 St Benet's Abbey

39 Friary, Burnham Norton

APPENDIX 4
✤ CASTLE AND TOWN GATES ✤

THE MAIN GATE of a castle or town had three important functions.
The first was defence, the second was control – to monitor all who
entered and to collect tolls on goods being brought to market – and
the third was to display the power and wealth of the town. Although
most large houses and monasteries were walled and gated, only the
gates of castles, town walls and the great houses can be considered
serious works of defence. A castle or walled town was likely to be
attacked by an organised armed force rather than an angry mob or band
of brigands. As the threat was much greater so was the architectural
response. A castle or town gate was closed with

38 Bailey Gate, Castle Acre

stout doors, usually strengthened by a portcullis with a drawbridge in
front. To bring fire to bear on the doors, the gate was usually flanked
by two projecting towers with loopholes – at first for bows and later
for handguns. There were often machicolations (or overhanging
battlements) so rocks, boiling oil or lime could be dropped on the
heads of the attackers. Some gates had a barbican as well. This was
an outwork consisting of two walls projecting from the gate to form
a long corridor with a further set of doors at the outer end.

51 Caister Castle

Only Norwich and Castle Rising castles and the principal gates in
the town walls at Norwich, Yarmouth and King's Lynn had all these
features. The lesser town gates consisted of a single square tower with
no flanking turrets but sometimes a barbican. The great houses built in the late fifteenth
century, like Oxburgh and Middleton Towers, needed effective defences though not on
the scale of a castle or town. Most of the defensive effort was lavished on the gatehouse
which had the usual layout of flanking turrets and loopholes and a drawbridge. By the
beginning of the sixteenth century no new houses were built with genuine fortified gates,
although stylised versions with flanking towers and crenellations like St Mary's Hall
continued the tradition.

32 Middleton Towers

APPENDIX 5
✤ INSTITUTIONS AND INDUSTRY ✤

EVERY INSTITUTION needs to keep some people in and others out. Until the false optimism of the 1960s nearly every school, hospital and factory was surrounded by a wall or fence with a gate. Most factory gates were simple without arches but where the gate was in the facade of the building it was given an architectural treatment. The best factory gates in Norfolk still remaining are those of the former Norvic shoe factory in Colegate, Norwich, with its pediment and tower and the Romanesque gate of the former Coop factory in Mountergate.

Military installations were always walled and gated and the two barracks in Norwich both had imposing gates. The barracks in Yarmouth and Gorleston did not have arched gates but ones flanked by lodges. None of these were defensible. Only the North and South Batteries, built at Yarmouth in 1782, had truly defensible gates, with entry gained through a wooden blockhouse.

56 Norvic factory, Norwich

The airfields built in the 1930s had elegant iron gates between brick pillars but their purpose was mainly decorative. The radar stations at Stoke Holy Cross and West Beckham had more utilitarian gates and were surrounded by tall steel fences flanked by pillboxes which made them truly defensible enclosures. The airfields were too big to be fenced even in wartime but were defended by pillboxes and trenches. It was only in the 1980s, with the threat of terrorism, that airfield gates were fortified anew with modern pillboxes that look like giant drainpipes and concrete blocks to impede traffic.

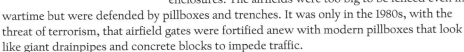

49 RAF Neatished

There are still plenty of institutional gates in Norfolk but high walls have given way to chain link fencing with automatic barriers substituted for gates. The principles of security remain the same but the element of display embodied in a fine piece of architecture is now confined to a logo or corporate sign. 🏠

Unilever, Bracondale, Norwich

GAZETTEER

Each entry has an Ordnance Grid Reference followed by its postcode.
The entries in *italics* are those shown only on the map at the front of the book.
Those printed in this colour have been demolished.

Town Walls

1   The East Gate, King's Lynn. No remains but adjoining stretch of wall.
    TF 6235 2036 PE30 1PP
2   The South Gate, King's Lynn. Limited public opening. TF 6219 1915 PE30 5SX
20 Caistor St Edmund. Public access at all times. TG 2306 0340 NR14 8QL
22 The North Gate, Great Yarmouth. No remains but adjoining stretch of
    wall. TG 5237 0818 NR30 1BG
25 The South Gate, Great Yarmouth. No remains but adjoining stretch of
    wall. TG 5254 0671 NR30 3LD
26 *Saint Anne's Fort, King's Lynn.* Can be seen from the car park of the Dock Office.
    TF 6180 2054 PE30 2EU
27 *Guanock Gate, King's Lynn.* Public access from The Walks. TF 6246 1972 PE30 1PE
38 *Bailey Gate, Castle Acre.* Public access. TF 8172 1515 PE32 2AG

27 Guanock Gate,
King's Lynn

Castles and Fortified houses

3   St Mary's Hall, Wiggenhall. Private. Not visible from the road. TF 5845 1451 PE34 3EJ
4   Inner Bailey Gate, Castle Rising. English Heritage. Open daily. TF 6630 2477 PE31 6AH
6   Oxburgh Hall. National Trust opening hours. TF 7404 0127 PE33 9PS
10 Baconsthorpe Castle. Free access during daylight. TG 1211 3816 NR25 6LN
8   East Barsham Manor. Private but easily seen from the B1105. TF 9165 3387
    NR21 0LH
31 *Denver Hall Gatehouse.* Private but can be seen from Ely Road. TF 6158 0157
    PE38 0DW
32 *Middleton Towers.* Private wedding venue. TF 6690 1756 PE32 1EE
35 *Hunstanton Hall.* Private. Cannot be seen from road. TF 6911 4184 PE36 6JS
48 Waxham Hall. The gate is accessible from Church Road. TG 4396 2623 NR12 0DY
51 *Caister Castle.* Private museum: Check opening times. TG 5048 1229 NR30 5SN
58 *Claxton Castle, Claxton.* Private, visible from The Street. TG 3351 0381 NR14 7AS
60 *Hales Hall.* The gate can be viewed from a footpath. TM 3688 9606 NR14 6QW

60 Hales Hall

Abbeys and Priories

5   Pentney Priory. Limited public access. TF 7007 1209 PE32 1JT
9   Walsingham Priory. Private. Access from High Street. TF 9341 3681 NR22 6BP
12 Thetford Priory. Public access. TL 8653 8336 IP24 1BB
17 The Bishop's Gate, Norwich. Private. Can be viewed from outside. TG 2347 0906 NR3 1RY
18 The Erpingham Gate, Norwich. Public access but closed at 10.30pm. TG 2335 0886 NR1 1HF
19 St Ethelbert's Gate, Norwich. Public access but closed at 10.30pm. TG 2340 0876 NR1 4DR
28 *Austin Friars Gate, King's Lynn.* In wall in Austin Street. TF 6185 2038 PE30 1DZ
29 *Whitefriars Gate, King's Lynn.* Open access. TF 6185 1939 PE30 5AF
36 *West Acre Priory.* Public access beside the church. TF 7804 1523 PE32 1UB
37 *Castle Acre Priory.* English Heritage opening hours. TF 8137 1494 PE32 2XD

47 Broomholm Priory, Bacton

39   *Friary, Burnham Norton*. Access from Friars' Lane. TF 8387 4281 PE31 8JA
42   *Binham Priory*. Public access. TF 9820 3998 NR21 0DQ
47   *Broomholm Priory, Bacton*. Private but accessible from the road. TG 3461 3319 NR12 0HA
50   *St Benet's Abbey*. Public access at all times. TG 3802 1578 NR1 1RY
55   *The Water Gate, Norwich*. Accessible from the Riverside Walk. TG 2389 0874 NR1 4DZ

Prisons

16   Norwich City Gaol. No remains. Catholic Cathedral occupies the site. TG 2233 0854 NR2 2PA
43   *Wayland Prison*. Cannot be seen from the public road. TL 9391 9880 IP25 6RL
52   *Sir John Soane's County Gaol of 1793*. TG 2323 0846 NR1 3JU
53   *Norwich Prison of 1827*. Gate is the entrance of the Castle Museum.
     TG 2323 0846 NR1 3JU
54   *Norwich Prison of 1887*. The gate can be seen from Knox Road. TG 2457 0959
     NR1 4LU
30   Town Gaol, King's Lynn. Open to the public. TF 6172 1986 PE30 5DQ

53 Norwich Prison of 1827

Factories and Breweries.

23   Lacon's Brewery, North Quay, Great Yarmouth. Now a supermarket.
     TG 5215 0799 NR30 1J2
56   *Norvic shoe factory*. The gate can be seen from Colegate. TG 2299 0900 NR3 1DD
57   *Co-op shoe factory*. The gate is in Mountergate. TG 2351 0834 NR1 1PW

Barracks

15   Britannia Barracks, Norwich. The gate is accessible from Britannia Road.
     TG 2351 0952 NR1 4HP
49   RAF Neatished, Horning. Museum with limited opening. TG 3459 1852
     NR12 8YB

57 Co-op shoe factory,
Norwich

Park Gates

33   *South Lodge, Hillingdon*. Seen from A148. TF 7179 2556 PE31 6BL
34   *East Lodge, Hillingdon*. Seen from B1153. TF 7279 2621 PE31 6DT
40   *North Gate, Holkham*. Public access. TF 8916 4352 NR23 1RH
41   *Palmer's Lodge, Holkham*. Private. Can be glimpsed from the Golden Gates. TG 9024 4186 NR23 1SF
44   *Nunnery Gate, Thetford*. Open access. TL 8718 8227 IP24 3EN
45   *Grange Lodge, Heydon*. Can be viewed from the road. TG 1147 2709 NR11 6RB
46   *Hanworth Lodge, Gunton*. Private. Can be seen from the road. TG 2209 3358 NR11 7HQ
59   *Chedrave Lodge, Langley*. Can be seen from the Norwich Road. TG 3524 9941 NR14 6BG

Triumphal Arches and Entrances

7   Triumphal Arch, Holkham. Private. Easily seen from the Wells Road. TF 8824 3944 NR23 1RU
11   Stable Court Gate, Sennowe Park. Private. TF 9814 2557 NR20 5PB
13   Lych Gate, Kilverston. Public access. TL 8938 8401 IP24 2US
14   Scole Inn Sign. No remains. TM 1493 7890 IP21 4DR
21   Westwick Arch. The two lodges survive on either side of the B1150. TG 2814 2551 NR10 5BP
24   Wellington Arches, Great Yarmouth. Public access. TG 5301 0685 NR30 3AQ

45 Grange Lodge, Heydon

BIBLIOGRAPHY

Blomefield, F., *An Essay towards a Topographical History of the County of Norfolk*. 11 vols, London, 1805–10.

Cotman, Alec M. and Hawcroft, Francis W., *Old Norwich: A Collection of Paintings, Prints & Drawings of an Ancient City*. Norwich, 1961.

Davies, J.A., *Venta Icenorum: Caistor St Edmunds Roman Town*. Norwich, 2001.

Edwards, Derek and Williamson, Tom, *Norfolk Country Houses from the Air*. Stroud, 2000.

Emery, Anthony, *Greater Medieval Houses of England and Wales 1300–1500*, vol 2. Cambridge, 2000.

Harrod, Wilhelmine and Linnell, The Revd C.L.S., *Shell Guide to Norfolk*. London, 1966.

Hillen, H.J., *History of the Borough of King's Lynn*. 2 vols, Norwich and London, 1907.

Kent, Peter, *Fortifications of East Anglia*. Lavenham, 1988.

Kenyon, J.R., 'Early artillery fortifications in England and Wales', *Archaeological Journal* 138 (1981).

L'Estrange, John, *The Eastern Counties Collectanea*. Norwich, 1872.

Norfolk Record Office. *Plans, sections and elevations of the new Norwich Gaol*, NCR Case 16e/31 and NCR Case 16e/99.

Norfolk Record Office, *Report Book of the Victoria Building Company*, BR 185/3

Palmer, C.J., *The Perlustration of Great Yarmouth*. 3 vols. Great Yarmouth, 1875.

Pevsner, Nikolaus and Wilson, Bill, *The Buildings of England. Norfolk 1: Norwich and North-East*. London, 1997.

Pevsner, Nikolaus and Wilson, Bill, *The Buildings of England. Norfolk 2: North-West and South*. London, 1997.

Rice, Matthew, *Building Norfolk*. London, 2008.

Rye, Walter, *A History of Norfolk*. London, 1885.

Smith, T.P., 'The Medieval town defences of King's Lynn', *Journal of British Archaeology* 33 (1970).

Turner, Hilary L., *Town Defences in England and Wales*. London, 1970.

The Victoria History of the Counties of England. *Norfolk*. 2 vols, London, 1906.

Wade-Martins, Peter, *An Historical Atlas of Norfolk*. Norwich, 1993.

Wright, J.A., *Brick Buildings in England*. London, 1972.

35 Hunstanton Hall. The fifteenth century gatehouse viewed through a seventeenth century arch.